WHEN THE BLUEGRASS RAN RED

The Era when Bowling Green was "Little Chicago," Newport was "Sin City," and Sensational Crime, Corruption and Murder were Rampant across Kentucky

WES SWIETEK

AP™
Acclaim Press
MORLEY, MISSOURI

Acclaim Press
— Your Next Great Book —
P.O. Box 238
Morley, MO 63767
(573) 472-9800
www.acclaimpress.com

Book Design: Ron Eifert
Cover Design: Frene Melton

ISBN: 978-1-965370-29-2 | 1-965370-29-2
Library of Congress Control Number: 2025945116

First Printing 2025
Printed in the United States of America
10 9 8 7 6 5 4 3 2 1

This publication was produced using available information.
The publisher regrets it cannot assume responsibility for errors or omissions.

CONTENTS

DEDICATION

As always, for Molly, Will and Mary Anna

AUTHOR'S NOTE

Versions of some of the following chapters were first published in the *Bowling Green Daily News.*

PROLOGUE

In the early 1900s, a place known as Burke's Alley became the epicenter of crime in the small but growing river town of Bowling Green, Kentucky. The narrow alley was just a few blocks long, in the less desirable area of town, but it was also just one block from the bustling Louisville and Nashville Railroad depot and the city's downtown.

The Barren River flowed peacefully nearby, but the Alley was a turbulent, churning mix of violence, poverty, vice and crime.

There was a mix of brick buildings with tiny apartments and crumbling, makeshift shacks lining the Alley. The entryway to the Alley was called "The Hole in the Wall" — a dark, narrow passage between two large brick buildings.

The passageway emerged into a large, trash-strewn courtyard with small, crumbling shacks on either side. A pungent smell came not only from the trash but the building in the middle of the courtyard that served as a communal bathroom for dozens of families.

As countless trains pulled into the nearby depot, visitors to the Alley could avail themselves of nearly any vice imaginable, from moonshine to gambling and prostitution. A blind "preacher" was one of the city's most notorious bootleggers and operated out of Burke's Alley.

Whenever a crime occurred in the city, police invariably descended on the Alley to search for suspects. While the only "crime" most Burke's Alley residents were guilty of was being poor, there were also plenty of career criminals who lived in and operated out of the Alley.

Murders, assaults, gambling, prostitution and other crimes became commonplace in Burke's Alley at a rate few today could comprehend.

In the 1960s, when Burke's Alley was slowly scraped away in the name of urban renewal — buildings torn down and never rebuilt and streets realigned — there was the belief that the effort would curb crime in the city.

That belief would soon be shattered.

Not only were there numerous high-profile crimes across Kentucky in the 1960s and early 1970s that are still discussed today, but Bowling Green also became known for vice and crime — so much so that the city earned the nickname "Little Chicago."

It was generally assumed that the Little Chicago nickname was pinned on Bowling Green in the 1960s and that this was the beginning of large-scale lawlessness in the city.

However, the largely forgotten record of Burke's Alley tells another story of how alleged corruption and criminal enterprises had drawn comparison between Bowling Green and the Windy City decades earlier.

In 1931, a group calling itself the New Council Campaign Committee ran large ads in the *Bowling Green Daily News* urging residents to vote for new city leaders.

"Is Bowling Green to become more of a 'Little Chicago' with 'gangs' and 'racketeering' increasing," the ad asked in bold letters.

The ad referenced the recent election loss in Chicago of "Big" Bill Thompson as mayor. Thompson was a notoriously bombastic mayor with close ties to the man who many felt really ran the city — Alphonse Gabrial Capone.

The ad laid out explicit claims against an unnamed individual it claimed was pulling the strings behind the scenes at Bowling Green's picturesque city hall; that city jobs were handed to his allies, alcohol was being sold through his business (this was during Prohibition), and police were being corrupted. "He is the Al Capone of Bowling Green," according to the ad.

While alleged corruption in city government was not explicitly discussed at the time on the pages of the city's newspapers, there was a general understanding that corrupt forces were at play.

A typical political platform from the early twentieth century was offered by a candidate (and future Bowling Green mayor) named Henry E. Stone in 1921.

The lengthy platform included avoiding "political favoritism," not giving city business to elected officials, and that "the city shall be freed of the large and growing criminal element which has been permitted to gather here unmolested."

In the city commission race two years later, the *Daily News* reported that there were widespread reports of thousands of dollars being spent on illegal vote buying "with little or no effort … to conceal the fact."

While the paper called for the prosecution of those involved, they apparently never were.

The following decades saw some notorious crimes — including the infamous "Murder Mansion" double murder of 1948 — along with periods of relative tranquility.

Although it ebbed and flowed, crime in Bowling Green had been ever-present since nearly its founding.

The wave of crime, however, turned into a tsunami in the 1960s and early 1970s.

But Bowling Green was not alone in seeing a rise in sensational crimes, and the Bluegrass has had more than its fair share of notorious characters and cases since its founding in 1792. In fact, a pair of brothers who were reportedly America's first serial killers left a trail of bodies in Kentucky in its earliest years.

The Harpe brothers, Micajah and Wiley, were reportedly born in North Carolina in the mid- to late 1700s. Sources disagree on the exact dates, and some writers even claim the Harpes were cousins born in Scotland. Whatever their origins, Micajah eventually became known as "Big Harpe" and the smaller Wiley was thus known as "Little Harpe."

In 1894, the *Bowling Green Democrat* ran a lengthy article about the Harpes. Big Harpe was described as "a perfect giant in strength and build."

Wiley's smaller stature was not, however, an impediment to his activities. One newspaper in 1890 described him as being as "agile and wiry as the mountain panther."

Few other descriptions of the brothers would be so kind.

One illustration of the Harpe brothers from the time shows two men who look more like beasts then they do humans. And it's no wonder. While the Harpe brothers are largely forgotten today, they were called by the Bowling Green newspaper "inhuman fiends" and "the bloodiest criminals that ever darkened the pages of Kentucky's history."

It is speculated the Harpe brothers killed as many as 50 victims — some for money but perhaps even more as a result of pure evil — as they traveled through the region in the late 1700s.

The Harpes, alone or in cooperation with other criminal bands, reportedly engaged in every conceivable crime during this time. These crimes included everything from robbery to torture and murder and stretched from Southern Illinois to Knoxville, Tennessee and everywhere in between.

At one point, the Harpes reportedly joined with notorious river pirates robbing flatboats laden with goods on the Ohio River. There is also a popular tale of the Harpes pushing victims, sometimes tied to horses, off a high bluff to their death.

At some point, the Harpes were jailed in Tennessee for stealing horses, but escaped and went a murder spree in 1799 that ultimately led to Big Harpe's demise.

After escaping from the jail in Tennessee, the Harpes went north, entered Kentucky and seemingly killed everyone they came across, "sparing neither young or old, male or female, in their insatiable thirst for human blood," according to the 1894 *Bowling Green Democrat* article.

The Harpes reportedly tortured and killed two of their slaves for trying to escape. An elderly couple living nearby named Simpson were found in their cabin "with their throats cut ear to ear" — presumably two more Horrible Harpe victims.

An 1890 *Louisville Courier-Journal* article looking back on crimes that were almost a century old at that point, said the Harpes had just passed through Russellville when they came across the Titsworth brothers who were traveling with their families and some slaves. The Harpes attacked, killing men, women and children.

As the Harpes moved further north, they came across the cabin of a man named Stegall (sometimes also spelled Stegal) in Muhlenberg County. Stegall was away from the cabin at the time and the Harpes reportedly killed the seven remaining occupants of the cabin and set it ablaze.

When Stegall returned to the horrific scene, he quickly organized a group of men to pursue the Harpes.

A man named Lieper (sometimes spelled Leeper) was chosen based on his bravery to lead the hunt for the Harpes, which he did aboard a borrowed horse named "Monkey."

Lieper caught up to the Harpes at Pond River, which is a tributary of the Green River. A chase on horseback ensued with Lieper and Big Harpe in the front of the pack. Finally, Lieper caught up to Big Harpe and shot him off his horse. The injured Big Harpe was taken to a nearby tree and a noose placed around his neck. The *Bowling Green*

Democrat article said that before he was lynched, the men asked Big Harpe why he had killed so many.

His response, according to the article, was "because I hate the whole human race."

When he was asked why he also killed children — "because I enjoyed it," Big Harpe said. "I beat out the brains of my own children and do you think I would care more for the brats of strangers than I did for my own babes?"

The "infuriated listeners quickly swung his gigantic form from the nearest tree," the newspaper reported.

Then, "Stegal, the husband of the last woman victim, cut off the head of the lifeless murderer and placed it in the forks of the tree that had served as a scaffold, where it long remained, causing the place to be known ever afterwards as Harpe's Head."

"The body was left to be devoured by vultures and wild animals," according to the *Courier-Journal.*

In 1967, the Kentucky Historical Society erected a historical marker in Webster County to mark the location of what is still known as Harpe's Head.

Amid the commotion of his brother's capture, Little Harpe escaped.

Various versions were reported of what happened to him, but the *Bowling Green Democrat* article claimed Little Harpe fled to Mississippi and joined up with a notorious river pirate known as, appropriately, Miller the Pirate.

The alliance, however, did not last long. Knowing that there was a bounty on Miller's head, Little Harpe reportedly waited one night until the pirate was asleep and cut off his head.

He then presented Miller's head to the local sheriff and demanded the reward. The sheriff reportedly recognized the bounty-seeker as the notorious fugitive.

"I believe you are Little Harpe, who is badly wanted in Kentucky, and I will have to lock you up," the sheriff said.

Little Harpe was taken to Greenville, Mississippi for a trial, where he was found guilty and sentenced to hang. (Other accounts have Little Harpe being tried and executed elsewhere.)

According to one version of the story, Little Harpe was also reportedly asked about his motivations for the many murders and responded only that he "loved to kill."

As he "cursed his captors with the vilest oaths," Little Harpe took one more life. Rather than wait for the executioner to open the trap door, he jumped off the platform "and launched into eternity."

"Thus ended the dark career of two of the most mysterious and infamous characters that ever cursed civilized society," according to one newspaper article.

The wives of the Harpe brothers were also captured and taken to Russellville to stand trial. It was determined, however, that they were also victims of the Harpe brothers and freed. The 1890 *Courier-Journal* article said, "the two women remained in Logan County the rest of their lives. Maria Davidson, who lived until about 1845, married a respectable farmer and has descendants living in that county to this day."

How much of the Harpe tale, and their reported confessions, was exaggerated or made up entirely, remains unknown.

As to their Kentucky crimes, various newspaper accounts list several. Although with scant and sometimes conflicting detail, the commonly reported Harpe murders in the region were:

- April 12, 1799 — a coroner's inquest jury in Warren County ruled that Frederick Stump Jr. was murdered by the Harpes near Bowling Green. Not content with just killing Stump, "they disemboweled him and filled his stomach cavity with stones" and then dumped the body in Barren River.
- The Harpes killed a man named John Graves and his teenage son with axes somewhere in southcentral Kentucky.
- "Logan County" — the Harpes killed a young girl, a slave and an entire family — it's not clear if this is the same incident as the Stegal family murders.
- August 1799 — a few miles northeast of Russellville, Big Harpe allegedly killed his infant daughter by smashing her head into a tree after she wouldn't stop crying.
- The Harpes reportedly killed a young man (sometimes reported to be a slave) in the vicinity of Mammoth Cave by also slamming his head into a tree.

The Harpe brothers set a bloody standard for criminal activity in Kentucky's earliest days.

Fast forward to the 1960s and 1970s and from Lexington to Newport and the small town of Lewisburg, sensational murders, crime and corruption were again making daily headlines in the commonwealth.

While crime and corruption are, unfortunately, a part of every era in Kentucky's history, the roughly 1965-1975 period was especially fertile ground for sensational crimes. Colorful characters, along with rampant corruption and horrific violence, produced a unique period in the commonwealth's history.

Many of the murder cases remain unsolved. Those murders and the era of sensational, headline-making crime are still vividly remembered, discussed and written about to this day.

In the following pages, we examine some of the true stories from the era, when the Bluegrass ran red with blood.

WHEN THE BLUEGRASS RAN RED

The Era when Bowling Green was "Little Chicago," Newport was "Sin City," and Sensational Crime, Corruption and Murder were Rampant across Kentucky

Chapter 1

THE SILENT WITNESS

Richelieu Road in Barren County, Kentucky, is about as secluded as someone looking to kill could ask for.

It is sparsely populated and was even more secluded in the 1960s. The short, narrow road is bordered only by a few farmhouses spaced miles apart, fields of golden corn, beans, tall grass, and dense woods.

So, the bread truck driver, at his job early that spring morning as usual, was undoubtedly surprised when he found his path blocked as he made his way down the seldom traveled road that Wednesday, April 20, 1966.

At around 7 a.m., he entered a narrow stretch of the gravel road bordered closely by trees near the small Orange family cemetery. He came upon a station wagon parked awkwardly on the road, blocking his path. There appeared to be no one inside. He got out of his truck and approached the vehicle.

As he got closer, he saw a shape in the small ditch on the passenger side of the station wagon. He stepped closer and saw it was the body of a slender young woman with dark hair. She was motionless.

That's when he heard the crying.

He looked into the rear window of the station wagon and saw a small, curly-haired girl in the back seat with tears streaming down her cheeks.

❖❖❖❖❖

Shortly after the bread truck driver's grisly discovery, a school bus driver, Marion Dennis Graham, pulled up on the scene. She and the truck driver took the girl, who looked to be about 2, out of the station wagon and drove to a nearby home where they called Butler County Sheriff, J.V. McKinney.

It took the sheriff, in his first year on the job, just a few minutes to arrive from Morgantown, the county seat. The area was soon swarming with local and state investigators.

Butler County Coroner Charlie Brooks was the first to thoroughly examine the body. He determined that the woman, who appeared to be in her mid-20s, had been shot once in the head near the right temple and once in the heart, apparently by a .22 caliber pistol. It was clearly an execution.

The little girl appeared to be traumatized, but unharmed. Brooks estimated that the woman had been dead for at least 4 or 5 hours, meaning the murder likely took place in the early morning hours on Wednesday. The child, a silent witness, was left alone in the dark just a few feet from the body.

The 1957 station wagon had Warren County license plates. A short while after McKinney radioed in the plate number, he was informed that the vehicle was registered to Barbara Smith Crouse, age 25. The address on file was that of a small rental home on Route 6 in Bowling Green.

Brooks's wife Mildred arrived at the house where the little girl, whom police assumed was the dead woman's daughter, had been taken. She comforted her as best she could.

The woman's body was transported to a Morgantown funeral home, where an identification was soon made by Warren County Sheriff Christy Watts and deputy Charles Forshee. The men had interviewed Barbara Crouse a few months before in relation to a report she made that some armed men had stolen between $200 and $300 from her and her husband the previous November.

While processing of the crime scene continued, police learned that Barbara Crouse and her husband Robert Crouse, 32, along with their 2-year-old daughter Dotty (sometimes spelled Dottie) had recently moved out of the Route 6 house. The Crouses had checked in that Tuesday at a motel on Highway 31-W, just outside of Bowling Green.

Kentucky State Police Detective Guy McMillen, the sheriff's son, had meanwhile arrived on Richelieu Road and examined the station wagon. Inside were a large number of casings and shells from .22 and .32 caliber handguns as well as from a shotgun. McMillen was also able to lift a large number of fingerprints from inside the vehicle.

Later examination revealed that the trajectory of the bullets indicated Barbara Crouse had been standing and was relatively near her killer when she was shot. One bullet was still lodged in her chest and the other bullet was later found in the ditch.

There were no obvious tire tracks from another vehicle, so police were looking for one or more individuals with at least three guns who likely fled on foot. Dozens of law enforcement officers from Barren, Logan, and Warren counties, as well as from the state police, fanned out from Richelieu Road in search of the killer or killers.

Police told reporters on the scene that they were confident "of an early arrest in the case."

Despite the positive identification of Barbara Crouse by members of law enforcement who knew her, as well as the station wagon being registered in her name, the identity of the victim in the ditch was quickly put in question.

Numerous people contacted authorities in Butler County to report that the woman found in the ditch was likely a Bowling Green woman named Beverly Elliott, apparently based on a description of the victim in early news reports and the fact that Elliott was nowhere to be found.

One of those who identified the victim as Elliott was a Warren County Jail inmate named Henry Ray King. The 19-year-old had been arrested on charges of flourishing a deadly weapon.

To bolster his identification, he listed off several items he had given Elliott; similar items (which were never publicly disclosed) were found in the victim's purse.

Officials asked a dozen people who knew Elliott or Barbara Crouse to come to Butler County and identify the body at the funeral home; eight said they thought it was Elliott, four said they were sure it was Barbara Crouse.

Even a veteran of law enforcement who was an investigator for the commonwealth's attorney office and knew Elliott said he couldn't be sure it was, or wasn't, her.

The identification effort was hampered by the fact that the gunshot to the victim's temple had partially disfigured her face.

Out of an abundance of caution, Sheriff McKinney ordered that the victim's burial, slated for that Saturday morning, be delayed until they could positively identify the corpse.

Police finally tracked down Elliott's father in Indiana. They asked him to try and find his daughter's whereabouts and have her contact the police. Within an hour, Elliott called from Louisville, where she had been staying, to report "I am very much alive and kicking."

With police now satisfied that the body was that of Barbara Crouse, the obvious question was, where was Robert Crouse?

Police in four counties were actively looking for him. He was not at first officially named a suspect, but police obviously had many questions — if they could find him.

Robert's description was listed in statewide newspapers — about 5-foot-8, 145 to 160 pounds with a "ruddy" complexion and dark hair in his mid-30s. He was last seen by witnesses around 9 p.m. Tuesday night with Barbara and Dotty at the hotel they were staying at.

Police were now also looking for another man who likely was with the Crouses Tuesday night. When police went through Barbara Crouse's purse, they found several "pornographic" pictures of her in various poses. Some of the pictures also contained partial images of a man. The man, whose face was not shown, was described as probably weighing about 180 pounds; considerably larger than Robert Crouse.

When the motel room where the Crouses were staying was searched, they found "negatives" from an instant camera; the bath tub was also still partially filled with water, and one of the photos of Barbara showed her in a tub filled with water, leading police to assume the photos were taken at the motel. Since they had just checked in that Tuesday, the obvious assumption was that the pictures were taken that night, just hours before Barbara was killed.

There was more circumstantial evidence that there was another person staying with the Crouses at the motel — police found an order slip from a nearby drive-in restaurant. It was for three glasses of iced tea, three fish sandwiches, three pieces of banana cream pie and two boxes of fried chicken — much more than the couple and the toddler would need. Much of the food was found largely untouched in the station wagon.

Police also found some men's clothes in the vehicle. Some shirts were size 14 1/2 and would likely fit Crouse, but some of the shirts, size 17, appeared to be much too large for the slender Robert Crouse.

Also found was a bag of groceries containing cartons of two different brands of cigarettes — another indication that at least one other person was likely with the Crouses.

Sheriff Watts now confirmed that police were looking at a possible connection to the armed robbery Barbara Crouse had reported a few months previously. He said that following the robbery, Barbara Crouse had reported getting messages threatening her and her child. That might explain why, when the Crouses lived in the Route 6 house, neighbors would often see Robert Crouse driving back and forth in front of the home, scanning the road with a spotlight. The couple also routinely left lights on in the house all night.

Police also found out that Barbara's parents were dead and she seemed to have few known relatives. She had been raised by friends of her family near Macon, Georgia.

Robert Crouse was from the Detroit area and was a mechanic, welder and auto body shop worker, although he didn't seem to be working anywhere locally.

What brought them to the Bowling Green area was unclear.

Coroner Brooks and his wife Mildred, meanwhile, had been caring for Dotty. That Thursday, with her father still missing, she was turned over to the State Welfare Department until any family members could be found.

By then, Robert Crouse was more than a missing person, he was a murder suspect.

Chapter 2

WHERE'S THE HUSBAND?

As police continued to scour the area around the crime scene that weekend for more evidence, Robert Crouse was formally charged with willful murder, despite nothing but extremely circumstantial evidence.

By then, police knew that Crouse had a criminal record.

In fact, Robert Crouse had previously made headlines in his native Michigan for his criminal exploits.

The teenage Crouse lived in Center Line, a suburb of Detroit. Little is known about his upbringing there, other than from an early age, he developed a unique aptitude for theft — and escaping confinement.

In 1951, when Crouse was 17, he and a friend, Eugene Judson, 16, were arrested on charges of breaking and entering. They were sent to the Boys Vocational School in Lansing, but the pair seemed to spend more time away from the facility than in it. In June of that year, Crouse and the accomplice escaped — it was the third time Crouse had gotten out of the facility.

They stole a car in Lansing and drove to Shaftsburg, Michigan. They abandoned the car and stole another and headed for Center Line, where Crouse and Judson picked up a pair of Crouse's friends. They then drove to Detroit, where they were spotted by state police. They sped off, leading to a chase that ended when their car slammed into a ditch. Crouse and Judson ran into some nearby woods but were soon captured.

That fall, Crouse was given a one-to-five-year sentence for the auto theft to be served at the Michigan Reformatory in Ionia.

Almost a year to the date of his previous escape, the now 18-year-old Crouse walked away from a work detail at the prison's dairy barn. The escape defied logic in that Crouse was eligible for a parole hearing just a week later; The *Lansing State Journal* surmised that the warm weather put Crouse "in a vacation mood."

A $50 reward was offered for his capture.

While it's unclear whether anyone claimed the reward money, Crouse was recaptured after about a week on the run — again in Detroit. For his fourth (that we have records of) escape, Crouse was sentenced to serve an additional two to six years.

Crouse stayed out of the news until 1957. Now 24, he was serving his sentence at Jackson Prison in Michigan. Despite having served the majority of his sentence by then, the escape bug hit again.

He and another inmate wriggled through an 18- by 7-inch hole between cell blocks. A steam pipe was their only obstacle to the outside. They leveraged a wooden block underneath the pipe to give them more clearance. The other inmate managed to crawl through, but when Crouse was halfway past the obstacle, the wooden block gave way, pinning Crouse underneath the hot steam pipe.

His screams drew the attention of jail guards, who had to use a hydraulic jack to raise the pipe and free him.

News of the escape attempt was carried in newspapers across the country (and even Canada) with most highlighting the misleading angle that Crouse was "too tubby" to finish the escape. (One newspaper headline was "Fat chance to escape from this prison" — another was "Bob's too fat for freedom.")

The men were put in solitary confinement for their escape attempt.

There is then a gap in Crouse's story; we simply know he eventually quit trying to escape and was released from prison, met and married an attractive brunette named Barbara Smith, had a daughter, and moved to Kentucky.

❖❖❖❖❖

That summer of 1966, there were some rumors that Robert Crouse had also been killed, and in a fairly common scenario at the time, his body dumped in a river.

But police believed Crouse, and perhaps an accomplice, were likely still hiding out in the area. A farmer whose house was near the crime scene reported that while he and his wife were milking their cows that Friday, someone entered their home and helped themselves to some beans and cornbread.

At least two other area residents reported that, early on the morning of the murder, a man or men knocked on their door and called out, asking to use their phone. The residents said they never answered the door and thus did not get a look at the men.

Another area farmer said he had seen a man generally matching Crouse's description and wearing dress pants, a white shirt and jacket near the crime scene in a wooded area.

To see if the cornbread and beans thief was Crouse, police sent some fingerprints they lifted at the farmhouse to compare to those they received from Michigan authorities.

While they waited for the results, the manhunt continued with the Bowling Green office of the FBI, that was now also involved.

Police warned the public that they believed Crouse was armed and dangerous, and likely still in the area.

In the latter theory, they were — somewhat — correct.

On May 20, while William "Dick" Sullivan was searching for the herb ginseng, he saw something strange partially sticking out of a shallow sinkhole near Billy Goat Hill, about eight miles north of Bowling Green in the Garrett Hollow section of Warren County.

As Sullivan drew closer, he saw it was a foot.

Sullivan called the police, and when Sheriff Watts and others arrived, they realized that a man had been dumped head-first into the sinkhole and covered with three large rocks.

When the body was removed, decomposition was already advanced, leading to the assumption that the body had been in the sinkhole for several weeks. The face was too decomposed for an identification.

Warren County Coroner J.C. Kirby did a preliminary examination of the body, which showed it was the same size as the missing Robert Crouse.

The body was taken to the University of Kentucky Medical Center in Lexington, where an autopsy revealed the victim had been shot in the back of the head at close range — likely with a 12-gauge shotgun while he was standing or kneeling.

Another execution.

The state police lab was able to lift fingerprints from the corpse and make a positive identification — Robert Crouse had been found, about 20 miles from where his wife had been murdered a month earlier.

The autopsy showed that Robert Crouse had some undigested food in his stomach — including fish, chicken and banana cream pie. That matched the food the Crouses had picked up at the Bowling Green restaurant around 4 p.m. April 19. Because the food would have been almost completely digested in about 5 hours, police assumed Robert and Barbara Crouse had been killed around the same time — late on the night of April 19 or the early morning of April 20.

Two sheets — one full-sized and a smaller one that could have come from a baby's crib — were found near the sinkhole, leading police to theorize that Crouse had been killed elsewhere and wrapped in the sheets so his body could be carried to the sinkhole. Crouse's pockets were empty, save for a handkerchief.

Police assumed the killer was from the area, as the sinkhole was extremely secluded. Because of the weight of the three rocks on the body — estimated at a combined 350 pounds — they also concluded that two men, or one who was very strong, had dumped and covered the body.

Police then focused on the Crouses' movements in the weeks before their murder.

They learned that they had been staying in Louisville for the previous two months with friends before returning to Bowling Green April 17. The couple was apparently broke, and Robert Crouse appeared to be extremely nervous. His friends said he seldom slept and constantly paced the floor.

When the couple returned to Bowling Green, the Crouses apparently had come into a large amount of cash — although none was found on their bodies.

Police also theorized that Robert Crouse's body was deliberately hidden while Barbara's was left in the open so that police would be preoccupied with a manhunt for the husband while the real killer or killers made their escape.

If that was the plan, it had apparently worked.

While the discovery of Robert Crouse's body left police at square one in terms of a suspect in the (now) double murder case, it fueled the theory that the Crouses were involved in another notorious Kentucky case — the disappearance of a respected elderly banker and his adult daughter.

Chapter 3

THE CASE THAT BAFFLED KENTUCKY

A veteran police detective later called it "the most mystifying and senseless crime to be committed in this area."

And it started with a mystery.

In December 1965, Edgar Harper was 81 years old and still carried the title (even though he was mostly a retired figurehead) of president of the local bank in Lewisburg, a community of a few hundred residents nestled in the heart of rural Logan County.

Tobacco, livestock and lumber provided the livelihood for most county residents and Lewisburg was not an especially affluent community. But Harper was likely the town's wealthiest resident. He had been a farmer, teacher and mail carrier — until oil was discovered on his farm in the Quality community of Butler County. He now lived in a large two-story house on the outskirts of Lewisburg's small downtown, and everyone knew that aside from his shares in Lewisburg Banking Company stock, he had made good money from the more than two dozen active oil wells on his farm.

But Harper was anything but flashy. Although he was involved in various civic clubs and even ran (unsuccessfully) for sheriff once, he was described as shy and introverted.

His wife Zula had died two years earlier, and one of their five children, daughter Ella Givens, was Edgar's primary companion and caretaker.

Ella, 49, lived with her husband Eustice on the farm owned by Harper in Quality, about a 25-minute drive from Lewisburg.

Several days a week, Ella would stay with her father in Lewisburg to help with household chores, prepare meals, make sure he took his medications (six pills a day) for high blood pressure and a heart condition, and watch televised wrestling with him.

December 11, 1965 passed normally, with Ella leaving the Quality farm in the afternoon to spend the night with her father in Lewisburg.

Eustice planned to pick her up around 8 a.m. the next day from Edgar's house to make a trip to Bowling Green.

Early the next morning, Eustice called the Harper home several times to tell Ella he was on his way to pick her up. No one answered. Perhaps more perturbed than alarmed, Eustice got in his truck and started for Lewisburg.

When he got to the house, he tried to enter through the front door, which was typically unlocked when Ella knew he was coming. This time, the door was bolted, so he went around the rear of the house and entered through the unlocked back door.

That's when he noticed several unusual things in the house: a bathroom light that was always kept on had been turned off; there were two empty suitcases sitting in a hallway; and neither Ella's nor Edgar's bed appeared to have been slept in.

Strangest of all, his wife and elderly father-in-law were nowhere to be found.

❖❖❖❖❖

Eustice checked with neighbors and relatives about the pair's whereabouts, with no luck. Several people noted there were a lot of strange cars in the area that previous night, including near the Harper house, but that could be explained by a high school basketball game taking place in town. Eustice contacted law enforcement.

Police soon scoured the house for clues. They noted that Ella's car was still in the garage, a purse with about $8 in it was still in the house and, most disturbingly, Edgar's medicines and false teeth — items he never left the house without — were still there.

A kidnapping seemed the obvious scenario. Police contacted Lewisburg bank officials, who determined there was no money missing from or sign of entry to the bank over the weekend.

The only thing to do was await a demand for ransom.

Soon the Harper home was filled with relatives hovering near the phone waiting for a call from the kidnappers. Joining them were neighbors, reporters from across the region, and numerous law enforcement representatives.

As the disappearance made national headlines, the family offered a $1,000 reward for information, and volunteers and police scoured nearby creek beds, empty buildings, swamps and wooded areas.

"I've never seen anything like this case before," Logan County Sheriff Guy McMillen said. His son, state police detective Guy McMillen, was the lead investigator. With no leads, police asked family members, including Eustice, to take lie-detector tests. They all agreed — and all passed.

Family members told police that Edgar had reported to them some unusual recent occurrences. One was a phone call from a man claiming to be a member of the Internal Revenue Service saying he would be coming to the Harper home to discuss some bank business. The man never showed up. Another unidentified caller had asked Edgar to confirm he was the president of the Lewisburg bank. When Edgar confirmed he was, the caller abruptly hung up. On another recent occasion, a man came to the Harper house and claimed to be an FBI agent. He spoke to Edgar about some "bank business," he told family members, but there were no other details. The strange calls and visitor strengthened the suspicions of a kidnapping.

Adding to the frustration of police and the family were the hoax ransom demands — there were at least three in the first few days, including one called in to a Russellville radio station demanding $60,000. A drop off location was mentioned, and the money was left there — monitored by a dozen law enforcement officers. No one showed up to get the money and the call was dismissed as another cruel prank.

As four days passed without another ransom message, police openly questioned whether they were really dealing with a kidnapping. Family members also had to contend with the realization that it was unlikely that Edgar could survive this long without his medication.

Meanwhile, the volunteer searchers scouring the area for clues were joined by FBI agents, state police, and even an Army helicopter on loan from nearby Fort Campbell.

The effort finally paid off December 18 when a crumpled felt hat — confirmed by family members to have belonged to Edgar — and a pair of pantyhose of the type Ella wore were found in a rural area near the Wolf Lick Creek bridge about three miles outside Lewisburg.

Searchers then dragged nets through Wolf Lick Creek and scoured the adjoining land. They also did extensive searches of nearby Lake Malone, at some 900 acres the largest body of water in the region. But after almost a week of searching, nothing additional was found, and the search efforts were put on hold.

An agonizing Christmas passed for the Harper family.

On the last day of 1965, a Friday, a heavy equipment operator was clearing some land for a home site on rural Sportsman's Road in Logan County when he spotted a brown wallet in the dirt.

When he opened it, he found a Social Security card bearing the name of Edgar C. Harper. Edgar's son Edward confirmed the wallet was his father's.

The location where the wallet was found was near U.S. 431 — the main highway between Lewisburg and the county seat of Russellville. Search parties quickly formed and again scoured the area where the wallet was found, with no luck.

The found items, located some 15 miles apart, offered no real clues as to the whereabouts of the pair or to their fate.

Numerous tips, and the hoax ransom demands, kept police busy, and frustrated as all the leads were dead ends. One typical report came from a man who reported that on the night of the disappearance, he had seen two cars parked at the intersection of U.S. 431 and Peach Orchard Road in the White Oak Grove community. Police searched the area but found nothing.

Weeks passed with no new clues.

In mid-January, a newspaper reporter visited Lewisburg. He found a community on edge.

"There are doors locked in this town that never were locked before," a resident said. Mayor Marion Pitt said his hardware store was selling more door locks and bolts than ever.

More weeks passed with no developments, and it appeared the mystery might never be solved.

Then, in late March, a resident of Peach Orchard Road, Randall Adler, decided to enjoy the spring weather by going for a walk with his son. They wound up at the gravel road that forms a half circle around the small Martin family cemetery (some reports called it the White Oak Cemetery), where he spotted something next to a tree stump. He picked it up and discovered it was a part of some broken eyeglasses.

In the back of his mind, Adler had a question: didn't Ella Givens wear glasses?

He put the glasses in his pocket and went home.

Adler worked at the Emerson Electric Company in Russellville, where one of his co-workers was a neighbor of Eustice and Ella Givens. Adler asked the co-worker if Ella wore glasses. When the neighbor said she did, Adler gave the glasses to him. The neighbor in turn showed them to Eustice, who confirmed they looked like Ella's.

Eustice called Detective McMillen. To verify the find, McMillen took the glasses to Ella's optometrist.

Eustice didn't want to wait for the confirmation, so he and a friend went to the cemetery and began looking around. It didn't take long for them to find some handwritten notes about random business matters that appeared to be in Edgar's handwriting, along with a ballpoint pen.

McMillen meanwhile had confirmed with the optometrist that the glasses were likely Ella's.

He began organizing a search of the area for the following morning. At about 8 a.m., a few dozen searchers began fanning out from the hilltop burial ground. The small cemetery was surrounded by an abandoned farm, with thick brush, weeds and overgrown trees making for slow going.

A local farmer named Vane Brown, a close friend of Eustice's, was among the searchers.

About 200 yards behind the cemetery was a shallow creek bed, just a few feet wide, with a trickle of water flowing through the bottom.

As Brown approached the ravine, he saw something sticking out from under some brush-covered boards. As he got closer, he saw it was a white canvas shoe.

Brown later recounted to reporters what happened.

"Mr. Givens and me were walking about 10 feet apart when I seen a leg sticking out from under some boards," he said. "I yelled for the sheriff and then Mr. Givens come over and seen his wife."

Eustice, recognizing his wife's shoes, burst into tears. Ex-Sheriff McMillen (the newly elected Logan County Sheriff was a man named Gene Sweatt) shot off a few rounds of his pistol to summon the rest of the searchers.

A few men ushered the distraught Eustice to a car to take him home, sparing him of the gruesome scene that was about to unfold.

When searchers removed the brush and boards, they found Ella's body lying on her back. Animals and insects had ravaged much of her face and her left arm had been ripped off by an animal.

About 10 feet away was the body of Edgar, face down. His body, partially covered by mud, was better preserved than that of Ella.

Soon, reporters, photographers, and curious area residents surrounded the scene as news of the discovery quickly spread. Afternoon newspapers ran banner headlines about the find.

The bodies were taken to a local funeral home, where the coroner did a preliminary examination. Ella was only identifiable by the clothes she was wearing; Edgar was more recognizable. The coroner said he couldn't discern how long they had been dead, or how they had died. The bodies were sent to the University of Kentucky Medical Center to be autopsied.

Police meanwhile were scouring the area where the bodies were found in search of clues. There were the crumbling remnants of a small shack nearby, and police believed the planks used to cover the bodies were likely taken from there.

The area, based on the number of empty beer cans strewn about, appeared to have been a popular, although secluded, drinking spot. The new search unearthed Ella's wedding ring near where the bodies were discovered. There was also clear evidence that the bodies had been dragged through the cemetery to their hiding spot — some hair and a bit of material matching Ella's dress were found snagged on an old barbed-wire fence surrounding the cemetery.

Police theorized that the pair were killed in the cemetery and dragged to their hiding spot. The secluded location also seemed to indicate the killer, or killers, were locals familiar with the location.

The preliminary autopsy failed to determine how long the victims had been dead, but it did reveal the apparent cause of death – Edgar had a bullet in his neck while Ella had been shot in the head and chest.

Police assumed there could be more evidence at the old cemetery, but the problem was that the area had not been sealed off and many sightseers (one estimate was as many as 500), as well as searchers and reporters, had contaminated the scene.

But police lucked out in one respect — the road around the small cemetery had been re-graveled recently. Was it possible that some evidence lay under the new gravel?

Detective McMillen supervised as a bulldozer carefully scraped the top layer of gravel off the road. Sure enough, Edgar's glasses, and a pair of rusty .25 caliber shell casings, were found. The shells were matches for the bullets found in the victims.

Meanwhile, a more detailed autopsy revealed that Edgar and Ella had also been brutally beaten. Edgar had been struck on the head six times; Ella 15, by a blunt, hard object.

The new evidence led police to believe that the couple had indeed been abducted with a ransom, or access to the bank vault, in mind. The beatings could have been an attempt to get the pair to reveal how they could access cash Edgar may have been hoarding, or the location of keys to the bank vault. (After the abduction, bank officials told police that Harper did not have access to the vault — something that abductors would likely not believe coming from Edgar).

Ella might have simply been in the wrong place at the wrong time. The autopsy could not rule out that Edgar had collapsed, or even died, from his heart condition before he was shot, leading the abductor or abductors to then dispose of Ella.

Who could commit such a brutal crime was a question "on the lips of every man, woman and child in Logan County and most of the state," wrote a newspaper reporter.

With no new leads, police were relying on performing lie-detector tests on anyone they could even remotely classify as a suspect, as well as re-interviewing pretty much every Lewisburg resident. A few locals had reported seeing, and in one case even chasing, cars on or near Peachtree Road the night of the abduction, but none of the witnesses could provide much identifying detail.

Police also sent cut branches that had been on the boards hiding the bodies to the U.S. Forest Service in Madison, Wisconsin, to try to determine when they had been cut. If the branches had been cut in December, it indicated Edgar and Ella had been killed soon after being abducted. If the branches had been cut more recently, it meant the pair was kept somewhere else — a second crime scene that could yield more clues — if they could find it.

The Forest Service reported back that it couldn't determine when the branches had been cut outside of a broad time range — another dead end.

The one-year anniversary of the abduction came and went.

In early 1967, The *Cincinnati Enquirer* ran a three-part series examining the case. Detective McMillen surmised that the killer or killers may have been known to Harper, who let them in the house. Eustice lamented that no one had come forward with information about the case. He had put up his own $1,000 reward for information; he said he hoped he'd have to pay it, even though it would "leave me broke," he said. The banker's estate, valued at over $100,000, had been split among Edgar's children.

Even as the case went cold in the ensuing years, it was not forgotten, not only among Logan County residents, but many local law enforcement officers who continued to chase down rumors and potential leads when they came up. Sheriff Sweat even personally drove to California to interview a suspect – a small-time criminal who was known to have been in Logan County at the time of the abductions.

Since the consensus was that the perpetrators were locals, there was a strong belief that someone in the community knew something. It was just a matter of getting them to talk.

In the election for Logan County sheriff in 1969, an upstart candidate named Jim Johnson won the seat. While Johnson was a former State Police trooper, he was best known for the car dealership he helped run. Johnson had campaigned heavily on a promise of solving the Harper-Givens murders.

Another member of law enforcement who was keeping an investigative eye on the case was a veteran Kentucky State Police detective named Leroy Poole.

At some point, Poole began talking regularly to a 20-year-old truck stop restaurant waitress named Carolyn Brown.

One of the things they talked about was the night of December 11, 1965. Brown was just 14 at the time, but was hanging out with older men, many with criminal records.

Three of the men, she eventually told Poole, were the ones behind the murder of Edward Harper and Ella Givens. She knew this, she said, because she was there.

❖❖❖❖❖

In May 1970, the Harper-Givens murders again made state and national headlines with the news that three men were being charged with killing the pair: Kenneth Delano Almon, 36, his brother-in-law, James Taylor Lovan, 36, and Alfred Finley Harvey, 25.

The latter two men were currently housed at the state penitentiary in Eddyville.

In 1966, six months after the Harper-Givens murders, the three men had been charged with the armed robbery of a grocery store in Murray, Kentucky. Harvey pled guilty, and based on his other criminal convictions, was sentenced to life in jail. While Harvey implicated Almon and Lovan as being involved in the robbery, there was no other supporting evidence of their involvement, and the two were acquitted.

A year later, Lovan was found guilty of various charges related to numerous thefts, including hog stealing, and joined Harvey in Eddyville.

So, while their criminal pasts made Lovan and Harvey unsurprising suspects, Almon's arrest was a shock in many respects.

At the time of his arrest, Almon was a respected science teacher at Webster County High School in Dixon. He had previously taught at Hopkins County High School, where all three men were from. He had attended Western Kentucky University and then graduated from Murray State University. He was married to Lovan's sister, and they had four children. Even though Almon was described as mild mannered, he could be imposing, at about 6-foot-3 and 245 pounds.

Reporters had been tipped off to Almon's arrest, and when he was brought to the Logan County Courthouse to face a judge, he was greeted by a bevy of reporters and photographers.

A reporter overheard Detective McMillen phone Eustice from the courthouse.

"I want you to know, before it is made public, that we have arrested one man and are charging three men with the murders," said McMillen, who then named the three to Eustice.

After the call ended, the reporter asked McMillen what Eustice's response was to hearing the names.

McMillen said it was, "I won't have to write them down to remember them."

Logan County Judge William Fuqua determined at the preliminary hearing that, with tensions still high from the double murder in Logan County, it would be safer to house Almon at the Warren County Jail in Bowling Green.

Days later, the three men were formally charged with two counts each of murder, kidnapping and armed assault with the intent to rob.

Because of the massive publicity surrounding the case, Fuqua agreed to move the trial to Hopkinsville in Christian County. It was later reported that Fuqua considered moving the trial to Bowling Green but was concerned about the crime wave engulfing the city at the time.

Almon had retained a Bowling Green lawyer named Currie Milliken to defend him.

While everyone awaited the trial, Milliken attempted to get Almon out on bond. During a bond hearing, County Attorney Jesse Riley testified that Harvey had confessed to the crime and to Almon's involvement.

Harvey then sought to publicly refute the claim that he had confessed. He contacted state newspapers and gave them jailhouse interviews professing his innocence.

He claimed he had never confessed, and he knew the source of the story to be a girl he had dated back in 1965 — the then-14-year-old Carolyn Brown. He said police had tried to get him to confess by confronting him with her claim that they were involved. But, Harvey said, he had not even been in that state at the time of the abduction. He was making his way back from California, where he had family, and was in Evansville, Indiana, the night of the abduction.

Reporters dubbed Harvey as amiable and popular. The tall, lanky Harvey admitted that he often ran afoul of the law, but "in all the trouble I've been in I have never hurt anyone."

He joked that the reason he once rented a room at a brothel was because "the rent was cheap and I had fringe benefits."

However, in one interview, he readily admitted a story that reportedly had been relayed to the grand jury was true; namely that once when he had been arrested on other charges, police found a sketched map of the small town on Morton's Gap, Kentucky, with the local bank highlighted. Harvey told police there was a plan to force the bank manager to open the vault and "then take him out in the woods."

While it was unclear who was in on the plan (which was apparently never carried out) the parallels to the Harper abduction were obvious.

Meanwhile, the fight to get Almon out on bail continued at various hearings. Milliken argued that there was not strong enough evidence against his client to deny a bond and brought a slew of character witnesses to one hearing. Prosecutors argued that releasing Almon was a risk — not a risk that he would flee, but a risk that he could eliminate any witnesses against him before a trial. Ultimately, Fuqua agreed that Almon should be allowed out on bail of $10,000. An uncle put up the bond and Almon was released after almost three months in the Warren County Jail.

The three men were to be tried separately, and prosecutors decided the first person to go on trial would be Lovan, who was represented by a Paducah attorney named William Scent, who had once been a U.S. District Attorney and was a well-respected litigator known as a skilled orator.

On December 1, 1970 — just a few days short of the five-year anniversary of the abduction — Lovan's trial, on the single charge of murdering Edgar Harper, began in Hopkinsville. The prosecution was led by Commonwealth's Attorney James Lyne along with County Attorney Jesse Riley.

After jury selection, Lyne outlined the case in opening statements. He said the state would prove Lovan shot Edgar Harper in the Martin Cemetery after the banker would not reveal where the abductors could get some money or valuables.

Lyne also mentioned Brown as being a key witness the jurors would hear from.

Eustice Givens was the first witness called by prosecutors. Givens testified that, a few months before the abduction, he and his father-in-law had seen a large white car with three men in it drive slowly up and down a dead-end road behind the Lewisburg house. Not only that, Givens said, he could positively identify them, five years later, as the three defendants.

Scent pounced on the fact that Givens had failed to mention the suspicious car in previous police interviews, but Eustice stuck to his story.

The next few witnesses over the course of the week relayed the uncontested version of events that led to the bodies being found.

After a weekend adjournment, the state's star witness took the stand: Carolyn Brown. The petite, dark-haired Brown was anything but the meek young girl her appearance indicated — a reporter would later call her "a salty, tough-talking slip of a woman."

Brown related that she had married two years prior, and her legal name was Carolyn Brown Hampton, but she still went by the name Carolyn Brown.

She testified that she and the three defendants had gone to Lewisburg as early as November 1965 with the intent to develop a plan to rob Harper. She said Almon, in his white Cadillac, was the driver.

"We looked Mr. Harper's home over, to see how to get Mr. Harper and Mrs. Givens out of the home and into the car," she said.

After that trip, Brown said they returned the night of December 11, 1965. This time, they had two cars — Almon's Cadillac and Harvey's red Mustang.

She said the quartet made several stops that night — an unidentified person's house, and once in Lewisburg, they stopped for a cup of coffee at a restaurant, visited another person's house she did not know and then went to the Wells Grocery store, where they purchased some food. Brown also said a woman at the Wells store gave her some safety pins because her pants were "about to fall off."

They made one more stop, Brown said, to the home of a local police officer " … to see what he was doing. If it was OK and he wouldn't be in the way."

They then left the Mustang parked downtown behind the Lewisburg bank building and all climbed into the Cadillac.

They drove to the Harper home and parked in the back. The three men were wearing black leather gloves, and each was armed with a gun as they approached the rear of the house, she said.

Lovan then kicked in the door and the four entered. They found Harper lying on his bed, although he was still fully dressed, she said.

"What in the world is happening," Harper said, according to Brown.

Ella was also found lying in her bed. Brown said Ella screamed "like when a man walks into a room with a woman when she doesn't have any clothes on … ."

They began searching the house for cash or valuables, with no luck, and decided to leave with the pair after about 15 minutes in the house. On their way out, Finley grabbed some cans of food and a ham, Brown said.

With Ella and Edgar in the back seat, they left the Harper home. Lovan was in the back with them, Brown said, and he began slapping and hitting them in an effort to get them to reveal where Edgar kept his money. It's not clear how Edgar responded, but Brown said all they ever obtained was about $60 in cash from the banker's wallet. Brown said it was she who threw the wallet out of the car as they travelled the countryside.

They then drove back to Lewisburg to retrieve the Mustang.

Brown said she drove the Mustang to a rendezvous spot — the old Martin Cemetery on Peach Orchard Road.

Once there, Brown said Lovan took Edgar out of the Cadillac and began yelling at him about the money and then hit him over the head several times with a piece of iron pipe.

"The first time Mr. Harper was hit he fell to his knees. The last time he was laying on his back with his head turned to the right," Brown said. "There's a place where a child is buried there. A tombstone for a baby. Mr. Harper's head was almost to that place."

She said Ella was sitting in the car while this was happening but managed to get out of the car and began running. Almon quickly caught her and brought her back, Brown said.

She said she then saw Edgar Harper get shot in the head.

"Tell the jury who shot him," Riley instructed.

"Jimmy T. Lovan," she said.

"That's James Taylor Lovan?" Riley asked.

Her voice rising, Brown pointed at the defendant and answered, "James Taylor Lovan, setting right there."

She added that as Lovan pointed the gun at Harper, the banker said, "I'll give you the money if that's what you want."

She said that at the same time, Ella was begging Lovan to not shoot her father.

Brown said after the shooting she and Harvey left in the Mustang, with Ella still alive, to go to a planned rendezvous spot called Earlington Lake where a bootlegger the men knew lived.

Brown said she threw Ella's purse, weighted down with a rock, into the lake. Almon and Lovan then joined them at Earlington Lake – without Ella.

Brown testified that she later heard Lovan tell the others that the bodies of Edgar and Ella should be moved because they could be found too easily.

At some later point, Brown said, she heard Almon and Taylor tell Harvey they had moved the bodies and covered them with some boards and brush. The three guns were placed in a wrapped box and also thrown into Earlington Lake about a month later, she said.

Brown's stunning testimony only lasted 53 minutes, but at its conclusion, the judge ordered a three-hour recess before the defense would cross examine her.

As dramatic and detailed as Brown's testimony was, there was a problem with it, as defense attorney Scent was about to reveal during cross examination. While Brown's story, as presented to the jury, largely gibed with all the evidence, the issue was that she had previously told other versions of what happened that night, the lawyer claimed.

Scent told the court that Brown had told at least four different accounts of what happened, including an initial statement to State Police Detective Poole and an interview with defense lawyers in August when she said Almon and Lovan were not involved. There was another interview with defense lawyers more recently that also had contradictions to what she had just testified to, Scent said.

As the defense attorney pointed out the contradictions, Brown angrily responded that the version of events she had just relayed was accurate.

Scent also questioned Brown about her relationship with Poole.

Brown admitted she considered the detective a friend and would sometimes talk to him about personal problems.

"What kind of personal problems?" Scent asked.

"They're not before the court and none of your business!" she screamed.

Later, she said Poole was a "... friend. If you are trying to make something dirty of it, that is all wrong."

When Scent again pointed out contradictions in a signed statement she had given to the defense lawyers, a frustrated Brown yelled out, "You got me drunk and I signed them papers … what I said today was true."

Scent then questioned Brown about the official statement she had given Poole, suggesting that the detective had given her information on the case that she used in her testimony. He also again pointed out contradictions between the various accounts.

A rattled Brown finally blurted out, "Just about the time they were questioning me … I was on the bottle, drinking heavy."

Scent continued to question her about the accounts where she blamed, or exonerated, a variety of individuals.

Brown again blamed it on alcohol.

"When I'm drinking, I'm liable to tell you anything. That table will take up legs and walk," she said.

Court adjourned for the day, but Scent was not done with the state's star witness.

When court resumed the next day, Scent continued to question Brown about the contradictions, highlighting one of her statements where she said she and Harvey went alone to the Harper house and abducted the pair.

Scent asked her about her relationship with Harvey at the time.

"I would have stuck my head in the fire for him," she said.

He also homed in on her troubled personal life.

Brown said she was first sent to a juvenile detention center at age 12.

"How long have you been drinking," the attorney asked.

"Since I was knee high to a duck," she said. "As long as I can remember."

He then asked her how long she had been sleeping with men.

"As long as I can remember. That's why my daddy gave me away to the court and they took me. Because they couldn't do anything with me, Mr. Scent."

Brown also confirmed she had, at the age of 20, already been married three times. The first time when she was 14.

Scent then closed his grilling by asking Brown, "How long have you been lying under oath?"

Brown again yelled out, "I've never lied under oath! I've told you the truth and if you don't like it, I can't help it."

With that, Scent said he was finally finished with the witness, and the court recessed.

When it resumed, Riley called Brown back to the witness stand to try to salvage her vital testimony.

He told the judge he wanted to ensure that Brown understood what it meant to give a statement under oath. Over Scent's objections, the judge allowed the questioning.

Brown told Riley she had dropped out of school after fifth grade.

He then asked her what she understood being under oath meant.

Scent again objected, saying she had likely been coached on an answer during the lunch recess.

"I fainted after this morning," Brown responded to Scent. She said she had laid down in a back room during the recess with only the court stenographer present.

Riley again asked her what she thought being under oath meant.

"I knew I had to tell the truth," she said, further explaining that she knew that she had to tell the truth in the courtroom, as opposed to "... talking to a roomful of drunks."

With that, Brown's testimony was finally over.

❖❖❖❖❖

The prosecution moved on with its case by calling to the stand a man currently living in Louisiana, James Seay. (At various times in the trial, defense attorneys would ask questions of witnesses regarding the identification of Jimmy Seay — pronounced Jimmy C — as opposed to Jimmy T, which was one of Lovan's nicknames. The implication was that witnesses, especially Brown, were taking what they had heard about Jimmy Seay's alleged involvement in the case and attributing it to the wrong Jimmy).

Seay, who had become friends with Harvey when they both lived in California, testified that he had traveled with Lovan and Harvey in late November from the west coast to Kentucky. After they arrived, the trio went looking for a house in Lewisburg, which turned out to be Edgar Harper's house. He said Lovan went up to the door and talked to someone briefly, but he couldn't see who it was.

Seay said he didn't know the reason they went to the Harper house. He also testified that he had overheard parts of a telephone conversation where Lovan mentioned "a banker and his daughter," and checked out a swampy area near Lewisburg with Lovan and Harvey, where he heard the men discussing the location as a likely place – for something.

Seay said that, a few days before the abduction, he and Harvey had set out for California. They made it to St. Louis before splitting up, but Seay said he reconnected with Harvey in Fresno, California, on December 8 before again parting ways.

Under cross examination, Seay admitted he had never mentioned visiting a swampy area or overhearing discussion about a banker to investigators who had previously interviewed him.

Seay also admitted he had eventually been charged with stealing a red Mustang in Oklahoma while he, Harvey and Lovan were traveling from California to Kentucky. This was apparently the same car that Brown mentioned in her testimony.

Scent then referred to a transcript of an interview Seay had given to Riley. In it, Seay's description of the Harper house was initially vague. Scent asked if the interview was halted so police could take him to see the house in person so he could give a better description.

Seay denied this happened, but Scent noted the transcript included a notation by the court reporter that the interview was interrupted so a state police detective could take Seay to Lewisburg, for undisclosed reasons.

Seay also admitted that investigators had told him that he was facing potential charges of accessory to murder in the case, but no charges would be filed if he testified.

Another prosecution witness then testified that he had loaned Lovan $100 and in turn Lovan let him drive a red Mustang. Lovan later came to get the car and admitted that it was stolen.

An Earlington man named Kenneth Huddleston then testified — corroborating that he let Seay, Lovan and Harvey stay in his house in late November and early December of 1965.

A Lewisburg woman also testified, saying she lived in a home once occupied by the town marshal. She said on the night of the abductions, a man came to the house and asked, "if the cop was home." While she couldn't positively identify the man, she said he was in a white car that was occupied by a man and a woman.

Several residents of Peach Orchard Road told jurors that they had seen, or in one case heard, a car or cars driving quickly in the area on the night of the abductions. However, none could provide more than vague descriptions.

The next day, the fifth anniversary of the abductions, the state called its last witness. Joan Wells Harlow was 14 and working at the family grocery store on the night of December 11, 1965. She said she remembered selling cheese and bologna to two men she had not seen before that afternoon. She said she now recognized one of the men as Lovan. She was certain it was the afternoon of December 11 because she was scheduled to work at the concession stand at the high school basketball game that night.

Scent grilled her about how she could identify a man, whom she didn't know, when she had only seen him for a few minutes five years earlier. Harlow confirmed that prosecutors had given her pictures of the three defendants, with their names on the back, but she stood by her claim that she independently recognized Lovan when she saw him in court.

Scent then asked her a series of questions about that day, but Harlow was unable to recall, for example, who else came into the store that day and who was working with her.

The prosecution then rested, and the judge sent everyone home for the weekend.

When court reconvened Monday, it was the defense's turn.

Scent, who had deferred giving an opening statement, gave one that morning, outlining the main defense strategy — attack Brown's credibility. Scent said the defense would show that Brown "is a woman of easy virtue, not chaste — a common prostitute — and in Kentucky that is grounds to doubt the veracity of a woman's testimony."

Scent also said Lovan would testify.

The first defense witness was the city attorney for Madisonville, who said he knew the Brown family and testified Carolyn had a bad reputation and was not someone he would trust to tell the truth.

After that brief testimony, Lovan was called to the stand.

The defendant described an eventful life in which he had been married, and divorced, four times, has four children by two different women, and had split his time between Kentucky and California in recent years.

He freely admitted his criminal activity but said he had never hurt anyone.

He then recounted the days leading up to December 11, 1965.

In November of that year, he, Seay and Harvey were in California and decided to drive to Kentucky.

Along the way, they swapped cars for the stolen red Mustang before arriving in Earlington on December 1. They stayed at Huddleston's house where they passed the time playing cards, drinking and visiting a local bootlegging joint.

On December 4, Lovan said he purchased a 1953 Plymouth, which he used to take Seay and Harvey to Evansville so they could take a Greyhound bus back to California. He said he didn't hear from Harvey again until December 11, the night of the abductions. Lovan said Harvey called him from the bus station in Evansville, where he had arrived after making a return trip from California.

Lovan said he then picked Harvey up around 11 p.m. that night in Indiana and dropped him off in Madisonville, Kentucky.

He then returned to Earlington and stayed with his parents until July. Lovan said he had never been to Lewisburg in his life, had never met Carolyn Brown and had nothing to do with the murders.

Under cross examination, Lovan assuredly repeated the same story and denials.

Scent then continued his defense by presenting a written statement from a psychiatrist, who evaluated Carolyn in 1965 for the state department of child welfare.

The psychiatrist wrote that Brown was "a mental defective with a sociopathic personality."

Called next were several lawyers to poke holes in the story of prosecution witnesses.

Currie Milliken testified that upon meeting him, Brown asked if he was Kenneth Almon. She also carried a pint of vodka with her and could turn "almost violent" under questioning, he said. Milliken also testified regarding police records the lawyers had obtained showing that Harvey had been arrested on December 9, 1965, in Raytown, Missouri — seeming confirmation to Lovan's testimony that Harvey was on his way back to Kentucky.

One of Scent's associates, David Denton, said he measured the distance from where Eustice Givens said he was when he saw the defendants in a car sometime before the abductions and the dead-end road. It was more than 114 feet, he said.

A parade of character witnesses was then called to the stand. They all basically told the same story: Lovan was non-violent, honest and of good character (despite his many brushes with the law) while Brown was untrustworthy with a bad reputation.

One of those latter witnesses was an ex-husband of Brown's, an "elderly man" named Virgil Coakley. He said he married Carolyn just a few weeks after meeting her. He said he filed for divorce even more quickly, only two weeks after their vows, because he found out she was cheating on him with two men.

A significant portion of testimony then turned to phone records and testimony, which Scent argued, showed that co-defendant Harvey called family members collect from Missouri the afternoon of Dec. 11, corroborating Lovan's testimony that

Harvey could not have gotten to Lewisburg in time to take part in the abductions.

The prosecution then had an opportunity to call rebuttal witnesses. Several people were called to testify, but there was little new information revealed.

A couple who owned a grocery store outside Lewisburg said that one day about a month after the abductions, two "strangers" came into the store and then left in a white car occupied by another man. The couple identified one of the men as Lovan.

Scent's cross examination revealed that the couple had only come forward with their recollection the day before, and that they had been shown pictures of Lovan by police.

An Earlington bootlegger named Leon Brown (no relation to Carolyn Brown) then testified, saying he and Lovan had once gone to Carolyn Brown's house together — contradicting Lovan's testimony that he had never met her.

The last witness was Carolyn Brown's father, Delmer.

Delmer said that at some point in late 1965, his daughter had several visitors to his house. Even though she was married to another man, Delmer said his daughter was dating a man named "Harvey," who came to the house and was joined by two other men — Lovan and " … Almon, I believe his name was," Delmer said.

With that, the testimony ended, and both sides began preparing closing statements in the 18-day trial.

The defense went first, and Scent renewed his attacks on the reliability of Carolyn Bown.

"If you don't believe her, it is your duty to acquit James Taylor Lovan," he said, reminding the jurors that a psychologist called her a "mental defective" with a sociopathic personality.

"She has a horrible reputation as a woman and as a witness you couldn't believe," he said.

The lawyer then recounted the various versions of the story she had told, and her explanation that she was drunk.

"Never have I seen a witness whose testimony was so contradictory," he said.

Scent then questioned the accounts of other prosecution witnesses and a timeline that didn't fit (if one believed Lovan's testimony that he drove to Indiana the night of the abductions to pick up Harvey at the bus station).

To close, he circled back to Brown: "If you doubt what Carolyn Brown said about this case, if you doubt what other witnesses told … you should acquit Lovan", he said.

Then it was Lyne's turn. He immediately addressed the elephant in the room — his star witness' credibility.

"Carolyn Brown is not, nor do we pretend that she is, a paragon of virtue. If she belonged to the Ladies' Missionary Society or the Homemakers, she wouldn't be a member of this gang in the first place … but also believe her when she holds up her right hand, swears to God and says, 'that's the truth.' "

He then outlined the instances where witnesses had seemingly corroborated her testimony, such as when Joan Harlow said Lovan and another man came into her family store the afternoon of the abductions.

He pointed out that the telephone bills entered into evidence by the defense didn't show who made the collect calls from Missouri on December 11.

Lyne then attacked Lovan's character and mocked the witnesses who admitted Lovan was a criminal, but not a violent person.

He ended with a dramatic flourish:

"Ladies and gentlemen of the jury, in Edgar Harper's billfold that was found in the culvert, there was this little card that read: 'Let me live in my house by the side of the road, where the race of men go by … ' A week from today, on Christmas day, I pray that we can all go to sleep, after dark, in peace, knowing that we have done our best to make this possible; to live by the side of the road, in peace."

After instructions by Fuqua, the 11 men and one woman of the jury retired to deliberate at 2:15 p.m.

The hundreds of spectators that filled the courtroom slowly began to filter out, undoubtedly with the expectation that jury deliberations would last until at least the next day.

But at 4:43 p.m., a deputy sheriff entered the courtroom and announced the jury had sent word that a verdict had been reached.

When court reconvened, the judge read the verdict sheet and then announced the decision: "We, the jury, find the defendant, James Taylor Lovan, not guilty …. "

Lovan's family and friends in the courtroom, many with tears in their eyes, rushed to embrace him. Lovan also began crying, while the

Harper and Givens family members sat quietly, apparently stunned at the verdict.

As they filed out of the courtroom, Lovan went over to the jury box and shook the hand of each juror.

But Lovan was unable to enjoy the verdict very long, as he was quickly escorted out of the courtroom for a return to Eddyville to serve out the remainder of his three-year sentence.

Eustice Givens said he was obviously disappointed in the verdict, adding that he wished the jurors had been taken to the scene of the crime, the Martin cemetery.

"If they had seen what we saw, they might feel different about that girl (Brown) and what she said."

Later, some jurors spoke to reporters and generally confirmed that Brown's reliability as a witness was a barrier to conviction. Two jurors said they believed Brown was in fact part of the crime, but who else was involved was unclear.

Even though Lovan was acquitted on the charge of murdering Edgar Harper, there were remaining charges of kidnapping, assault and the murder of Ella Givens. Lyne indicated he intended to prosecute Lovan on those charges.

Scent asked that the charges be dismissed, arguing that to try him again would amount to double jeopardy. While a decision on that issue was pending, the state and Alfred Finley Harvey had reached a deal.

In April of 1971, Harvey pleaded guilty to simply robbing Edgar Harper and Ella Givens. In exchange, the other charges were dropped, and Harvey was sentenced to 15 years.

It was believed that the state made the deal to secure Harvey's testimony in any future related trials. For his part, Harvey escaped the possibility of being convicted of the murders and a date with the electric chair.

Officials openly told reporters to expect more trials — presumably of Lovan on the remaining charges and of Almon. But as months passed, there was no movement on the prosecutions. As late as 1973, Detective McMillen said there was still a good chance of prosecuting the crime.

But Harvey's robbery convictions would be the only ones in the Harper-Givens murders. Although the case remained open and police continued to investigate any new leads, no new charges were ever filed.

Lovan was not prosecuted on the remaining charges, and Almon was never tried.

In 1997, McMillen revealed an irony in the case: because of the high school basketball game taking place on the night of the abductions, the Lewisburg bank had kept its vault open so that ticket and concession money could be dropped off after hours. If the abduction was an attempt to get in the bank vault, Harper could have simply opened the main bank door for his abductors — something he likely was unaware of.

Today, there are few tangible reminders of the crime in Lewisburg. The largest building in the small downtown is still the Lewisburg Banking Company building. Like almost every other building downtown, it sits vacant and boarded up.

Badly faded signs in and out of Lewisburg offer a welcome to the "family friendly" town that is the "Purple Martin Capital of Kentucky."

While most of southcentral Kentucky is relatively flat, the roads out of Lewisburg start winding and twisting up and down hills and hollers. The one-lane Peach Orchard Road is still largely secluded, with large plots of farmland between occasional houses. At one of the higher points on the winding road is the small Martin family cemetery, still circled by a gravel road. While it sits directly on Peach Orchard Road, the elevation keeps the back of the cemetery, presumably where Edgar Harper and Ella Givens were killed, largely hidden. A drooping barbed-wire fence still separates the cemetery from the adjoining farmland — and the spot where the bodies were found.

Edgar Harper and Ella Givens are buried elsewhere, as are most of the other main characters in the saga, who seem to have lived largely quiet lives after the Lovan trial.

While the case is still regularly discussed, it seems extremely unlikely that there will ever be new prosecutions. The mystery of who abducted the banker and his daughter is likely destined to remain one of the state's most enduring mysteries.

Chapter 4

A CONNECTION?

Back in 1966 as news of the Crouse and Harper-Givens murders shared space in Kentucky newspapers, the cases were often publicly linked.

A May, 1966 *Daily News* article noted that both the Crouse and Harper-Givens murders "had police literally running in circles."

One theory of a link between the crimes was that perhaps the Crouses were part of the kidnapping/bank robbery plot and were then eliminated for what they knew.

State police detective Sgt. William Smith was among those investigating both the Crouse and Harper-Givens cases. He pointed out that Barbara Crouse's body was found about halfway between Bowling Green and Lewisburg. And Robert Crouse, with his criminal background and handiness with a blow torch, was a logical recruit for anyone looking to break into a bank vault.

Adding to the speculation that the cases were related were stories in the numerous true crime magazines that were extremely popular on newsstands at the time.

Front Page Detective magazine outlined the crimes, with an emphasis on the Harper-Givens murders, in an article titled "The case that baffles Kentucky."

Inside Detective followed suit with a lengthy article titled "Unraveling Kentucky's Knottiest Murder Mystery."

Both magazines featured numerous pictures, including photos provided by police of the attractive Barabara Crouse.

For some reason, the articles made no mention of the Crouse's child found in the car.

Despite the speculation, state police detective McMillen admitted there was "nothing at all" to link the cases but "pure speculation. Officially, we have nothing at all to connect the two," he said.

There was some news in the Crouse case when in September of 1966, three men — brothers Leon and James Glenn Miller and Sonny Lundy, were charged with being the men who robbed the Crouses of about $250 in cash and old coins in November, but the trio denied being involved in the murders.

Lundy, it seemed, was getting special treatment while jailed, with speculation being that he was cooperating with police in the Crouse case.

The *Daily News* reported in May that Lundy, 40, had a previous sentence to be confined at the state jail in Eddyville for storehouse breaking put on hold, at the request of local officials, for several months. When he did go to Eddyville, he was quickly brought back to Warren County, where he served as a jail trustee. That, the paper noted, gave him "the run of the facility and city as well."

Being a jail inmate, apparently, was also lucrative enough that Lundy purchased a 1959 Plymouth while, technically, incarcerated. Lundy was often seen driving around town in the car, which he usually kept parked at the jail lot reserved for employees.

He also paid a $250 cash bond for a friend who had been arrested. Local officials offered no public explanation for Lundy's unusually generous treatment.

Meanwhile, speculation that there was a connection between the Crouse and Harper-Givens cases continued for years, but the theory took a back seat to a major development in the Crouse case in the summer of 1968.

In July of that year, police charged a Smiths Grove man named Charles Richards with killing Robert Crouse.

Chapter 5

THE USUAL SUSPECTS

Charles Richards was a cousin to a well-known criminal character with a rap sheet as long as the Barren River named Finney Richards.

Aside from a wide-ranging criminal history, Finney had as many lives as a pair of alley cats. Police estimated Finney had survived an astonishing 18 or more shootings.

In 1948, when Finney Richards was just 22, he was operating a rowdy and unlicensed beer joint on Main Street in Bowling Green that was a frequent stop for police. After numerous police calls to the business, it was finally shut down. (He reopened it later.)

The enterprising Richards was also arrested that year for running an illegal gambling "punch card" racket.

He steadily racked up a criminal history for charges like storehouse breaking, transporting illegal alcohol, assault, traffic violations, carrying a concealed weapon, murder, larceny, public drunkenness, and many, many more.

In 1950, police investigators from Tennessee came to Bowling Green to interview Finney and his girlfriend, Sallie Hawkins. They suspected the pair of being involved in at least seven break-ins in Carthage, Tennessee, in one night in November.

Finney, who was working as a mail carrier, didn't appreciate being questioned, and promptly "slugged" Smith County, Tennessee Sheriff, J.D. Rollins. Finney and his girlfriend were arrested and charged with the break-ins, while Finney earned an additional assault charge.

At a subsequent hearing, the 200-pound deputy sheriff testified that the 150-pound Richards struck him with four "lightning fast" punches to the face. "He whipped me. I'll admit that," he said.

Finney hired famed Bowling Green defense attorney Rodes K. Myers to defend him.

A Kentucky judge eventually denied the request to extradite the pair to Tennessee on the break-in charges after several witnesses testified they had seen Richards and Hawkins in Bowling Green the night of the break-ins.

Finney then struck Rollins again — this time with a lawsuit. The suit claimed Rollins attempted to hit Richards with a black jack during the questioning. The suit also claimed the extradition attempt caused his job to be in jeopardy and was humiliating. He asked for $25,000 for humiliation and $1,500 for attorney fees.

Just days later, the assault charges against Richards were dismissed.

In 1954, police found a large moonshining operation on some property Finney owned in the Sandhill community, but he again had an alibi — he was serving with the U.S. Army out of state at the time of the raid.

The military service appeared to keep Finney out of trouble — for at least a few years.

In 1956, however, he was back in Kentucky and became embroiled in a "fracas" at his reopened Main Street bar, called Finney's Place, in Bowling Green. A man named Earl Mills took a shot at Finney, but apparently missed. Miller was charged with attempted murder.

Finney was also embroiled with a long-standing feud with his brother-in-law, Joe Steenbergen, that resulted in a series of Wild West shootouts.

It's not clear what started the feud, but the first indication of trouble came in 1962. Steenbergen, himself with a lengthy criminal record, got into an argument with a waitress at Finney's Place and hit her in the mouth. Finney intervened in the fracas and Steenbergen reportedly grabbed a knife. Finney grabbed a gun and shot Steenbergen in the head.

Doctors at the city-county hospital removed a .25 caliber bullet from his skull and Steenbergen survived.

Apparently, the men (temporarily) made up at some point and Finney married Steenbergen's sister, Eleanor.

In 1967, however, things soured again.

Finney and Eleanor went to the apartment of Finney's ex-girlfriend Sallie Hawkins. Steenbergen was also at the apartment. It was apparently not a friendly visit, as Finney was carrying a gun in his pocket.

At some point, Finney apparently was reaching for the gun when it fell to the ground. A fight ensued with Richards slashing Steenbergen with a knife. His brother-in-law, however, pulled his own gun and grabbed Finney's gun as well and proceeded to shoot Finney five times with both guns.

Richards was shot in the pelvis, chest and head and had a fractured jaw and arm. He was taken to the hospital and listed in poor condition, but he survived.

Steenbergen was charged with malicious shooting with intent to kill. Eleanor was also arrested and charged with being drunk in public (she later paid a $20.50 fine).

Finney eventually recovered and got out of the hospital. Days later, with his arm still in a sling, he walked into a Main Street bar apparently looking for Steenbergen. His brother-in-law was sitting on a bar stool when Finney walked up to him, pulled out a gun and shot him several times.

Steenbergen lunged at Finney and the two wrestled out the front door to the sidewalk in front of the bar. Finney fired another shot into Steenbergen and then walked off as his brother-in-law lay bleeding on the sidewalk.

When police found and arrested Finney a short while later, he admitted shooting his brother-in-law, but claimed he had only done so after Steenbergen reached into his pocket. "I thought he had a knife," Finney said.

Steenbergen survived; Finney was now also facing malicious shooting with intent to kill charges.

The first case to be heard in court was the one against Steenbergen. At the trial, Finney testified he didn't have a distinct memory of what happened — presumably because of alcohol consumption.

Steenbergen said at some point Finney pulled out a knife. He said if he hadn't shot Finney, he would "have cut my head off."

The jury found Steenbergen not guilty based on self-defense.

While Finney awaited his trial, he got into an argument at his Main Street bar with a truck driver named George Marvin Payne. Payne, according to Finney and some witnesses at the bar, pulled out a gun, hit Finney in the head, and then fired a shot at him. Finney responded by pulling out his gun and fatally shooting Payne.

Police clearly didn't believe Payne was the attacker when an examination of a gun that Finney claimed belonged to Payne showed it had not been fired recently, and when no bullet shell or bullet hole was found in the bar.

Finney was now facing a second murder charge, but his luck at avoiding the grim reaper extended to his luck with juries. Despite the contradictions in his story of what happened, a jury found Finney not guilty by reason of self-defense after just 10 minutes of deliberations.

Finney's luck, however, would eventually run out.

❖❖❖❖❖

Charles Richards also had more than a few brushes with the law: he was charged in 1966 with storehouse breaking and in early 1968 with abandoning an infant child (essentially, failing to pay child support).

On March 19, 1968, Charles Richards was admitted to the city-county hospital with a gunshot wound to his chest. The bullet apparently only grazed Richards, who refused to tell police who shot him.

It seemed Richards, 43, decided that was a good time to get out of town and he moved to Louisville, where he reportedly worked in a body shop.

That summer, police were on the lookout for Charles Richards after they received a tip about the Crouse murders, and when they spotted him driving through Bowling Green, they stopped him and took him to the county jail on a traffic charge.

The next morning, they served him with a warrant charging him with the murder of Robert Crouse. Police revealed then that Richards had been identified as the killer by a woman named Barbara Flatt Purkerson.

Purkerson, 27, said she knew Charles Richards was the killer because she was there when the Crouses were killed.

Police offered a partial overview of Purkerson's account to reporters, revealing that they had suspected her, for unknown reasons, to have some information on the case.

After police picked her up in a Bowling Green bar and began questioning her, she said she was with three men (only Richards was identified at the time) when the Crouses were shot and killed in Butler County.

Purkerson told police she begged the men to spare Dotty's life at the scene. A motive, and more details, were not publicly revealed.

Police did reveal that Richards was denying the charges, and claiming he had a solid alibi.

Sheriff's deputy Charles Forshee said Richards told police, "You'd better check and see where I was when this happened."

News of the arrest made statewide headlines and again sparked open speculation that the killings could be related to the Harper-Givens case.

A week later, Charles Richards was formally indicted by a grand jury on charges of willful murder of Robert Crouse. The same day, Finney Richards was shot once again.

❖❖❖❖❖

Finney at the time was living in a trailer park on Slim Island Road in Bowling Green. One of his neighbors was Walter Hale, 58, who worked as a bartender and also had an extensive criminal history.

Hale said he was invited to go to Finney's trailer around noon that day. Already at the trailer were brothers Glenn and Leon Miller, and Jack Whitt, who owned the Powder Horn gun shop in downtown Bowling Green. Everyone in the trailer had a criminal history, including of course the Miller brothers, who had been charged with robbing the Crouses.

A woman described as Finney's girlfriend, Brenda Anderson, was also in and out of the trailer that day.

Hale said Finney offered him some moonshine to drink. When he declined, Hale said Finney pulled out a gun "and pointed it at me and told me to drink."

At some point that afternoon, Hale said the four men in the trailer viciously beat him, leaving him unconscious. They "left me for dead on the floor of Finney's trailer," Hale said.

When he finally came to, he saw that Finney was passed out on the couch, but he didn't know where the other men were.

"I played dead for a long time and then crawled out of the trailer and went to my trailer, but they had already ransacked it and got my guns," Hale said.

But Hale also had a bolt-action rifle in the trunk of his car. He retrieved it and went back to Finney's trailer. Anderson was back outside the trailer and saw Hale with the rifle. She begged him not to shoot her.

Hale bypassed Anderson and entered Finney's trailer. Hale later said as Finney, awakened from his slumber, rose up from the couch, he shot him in the chest.

"I (then) drove to town and down Kentucky Street and Jack (Whitt) came running out of his place and flagged me down," Hale said.

"I thought Jack was my friend, and he said like he was surprised what happened," said Hale in reference to the beating at Finney's trailer.

Hale didn't believe him.

"I'll show you what happened," Hale said he told Whitt. "And I shot him."

Whitt, who was shot in the hip, would survive.

Police quickly tracked down Hale after the double shooting and arrested him.

While he was being fingerprinted and booked at the police department, Hale insisted on telling his story to a reporter, despite BGPD Detective Darrell Moody reminding Hale his attorney had told him to keep quiet.

"I want the story told and I want it told like it happened," he said.

Hale said he was not surprised by the attack on him.

"I knew something was up. Finney was trying to set me up to be killed. I've expected something," he said.

When asked what the motive was, Hale clammed up.

"They think I know something," was all he would say.

Charles Richards would have heard about his cousin's death as he sat in the Warren County Jail. He was soon joined as a suspect in the Crouse murders by an Indiana man named L.G. Washer, who was arrested on receiving stolen property charges in Butler County. Police acknowledged they considered him a suspect in the Crouse murders.

The same day of Washer's arrest, at a hearing for Walter Hale, his defense attorney tried to link the Finney Richards shooting with the Crouse murders.

The attorney questioned Brenda Anderson whether she had overheard a conversation at the trailer regarding "what they were going to do to Barbara (Purkerson)."

Anderson said she had not. She did admit Finney was upset about Charles Richards' arrest, and knew Purkerson was living in a motel "with some guy named Jim," but that was the extent of any link to the Crouse case raised at the time.

Police meanwhile submitted Washer to a lie-detector test in relation to the Crouse killings, but the results were inconclusive. The identity of a third suspect (presumably the three men Flatt had identified) was revealed to be a Butler County man named Norman Brooks. But after a warrant was issued for his arrest, police discovered Brooks had recently died of a heart attack.

Police were also still speculating that there was a link between the Crouse, Harper-Givens and Finney Richards murders.

The belief seemed to be that the people behind the Harper-Givens abductions included one or both of the Crouses, and they were killed because of their knowledge of the case.

But it only took weeks for the investigations to be sidetracked.

In late August, Purkerson apparently changed her story.

Commonwealth's Attorney Morris Lowe said Purkerson was now repudiating her earlier statement that she witnessed the killings. Investigators were apparently worried that she was coerced or threatened to change her story. Police were apparently keeping close tabs on Purkerson and reported she had been seen with local crime figures in recent weeks.

Seemingly to put pressure on Purkerson, Lowe sought to have her probation on a previous child abandonment charge revoked. Even before that effort was finalized, Purkerson was placed in jail.

Even with Purkerson's repudiation, the case against Richards was going forward. His defense attorneys asked for a deposition session with witnesses, including Purkerson and officials with the Crounse Company, a river towing operation. They intended to show that Richards was working on a tow ship called the Nancy B. at the time of the Crouse slayings.

During the deposition session, held in open court, Richards' defense attorney Joe Huddleston cut to the chase when Purkerson took the stand.

"In the statement July 27, you said Charles Richards killed Mr. Crouse. Is that true or false," he asked.

"That's false," she said. "The entire statement is false."

In cross examination, Lowe asked Purkerson how she could know details of the crime if she wasn't there.

She responded that she read some of the details in news accounts and "made up" some other details.

As for her motivation in lying, Purkerson said she was motivated by fear and anger.

"I'd been drinking. Someone told me Charles was in town and had a gun after me. I was scared and mad at Charles and told that lie," she said.

She said one of the people who told her Charles Richards was after her was none other than Walter Hale — leading to more speculation that there was more to the death of Finney Richards than was apparent.

Lowe homed in on the theory that Purkerson was now changing her story out of fear.

"Has anyone told you to change your statement?"

"No, only everyone's told me to tell the truth," she responded.

"Are you afraid of anyone?"

"I don't think so," she said.

Also testifying was a bookkeeper for the Crounse Corp., who said Charles Richards was working as a cook on the Nancy B. towing vessel on the Ohio and Green rivers from April 17 to April 24, 1966.

However, he admitted it was possible for someone to leave the boat when it was docked and get back on board later.

The captain of the Nancy B., Hugh Snodgrass, testified he didn't recall Richards leaving the boat during the period in question.

In light of the testimony, defense attorneys asked that the murder charge be dismissed, but the judge declined. He did reduce Richards' bail from $50,000 to $1,000, allowing him to walk out of the Warren County Jail after a month behind bars.

Lowe told reporters that the prosecution would continue as he believed Purkerson's initial statement.

"There are things in the statement she could not have known unless she was there," he said.

But it seemed Purkerson was sticking to her story — she was eventually indicted for obstructing justice based on her admitting (or claiming, depending on what one believes) she lied in her initial statement. At the same time, her probation on child abandonment charges was formally revoked, and she was taken to the state Women's Correctional Institution at Peewee Valley to serve her one-year sentence.

Richards, meanwhile, was not staying out of trouble while out on bail. In late October, he got into a dispute at a Bowling Green motel. He was arrested and charged with breach of the peace and flourishing a deadly weapon. He quickly pleaded guilty and was given a $50 fine.

But he did soon get some good news; with Purkerson's testimony irreparably harmed, the trial on the murder charge was suspended indefinitely, with a strong chance he would never be prosecuted.

That left Hale's trial as the next opportunity to perhaps shed light on the Crouse case.

While he awaited the criminal trial, Hale was also in court as a defendant with several others in a civil suit. Hale was working as a bartender at the Spot nightclub when there was an altercation with three men, who were allegedly stabbed (non-fatally) by Hale and others. A jury eventually awarded the men $74,000 in damages.

In late March of 1969, Hale's trial for shooting Finney Richards got underway. Hale was the star witness for his own defense, saying again that not only had the men beaten him, but he also said Richards and Whitt threatened to kill him and Purkerson.

Whitt testified and denied beating or threatening Hale. Purkerson was also called to the stand, but refused to answer questions, invoking her right to do so under the Fifth Amendment.

The jury of seven women and five men seemingly accepted Hale's account of self-defense, and acquitted him after only an hour of deliberations. Hale was later convicted by a jury of wounding Whitt, but the penalty was a meager $50 fine.

While the verdicts were anticlimactic, what drew much interest was the judge allowed hearsay testimony not directly linked to the Hale shooting about the bombings, Crouse and Harper-Givens murders and the still unsolved slaying of Billy Graham.

It was revealed, for example, that Graham's beaten body was reportedly kept in the trunk of a car and unveiled to certain people as a warning against talking, as Graham had about the bombings, before it was dumped in the river. Graham's rumored killer, according to testimony, was allegedly a former Bowling Green police officer named Willis Alford, who had since been killed by police after a high-speed chase.

There was also testimony that Finney Richards planned to kill Hale because Hale had gone to police with Barabara Purkerson when she identified his cousin Charles Richards as the killer in the Crouse case. One witness said Finney had planned to poison Hale at one point, and intended to kill him that day in his trailer before Hale shot him first.

Much of the shocking testimony was provided by defense witness Joe Steenbergen — the former brother-in-law, and nemesis, of Finney Richards.

There again was speculation that the Crouses were killed because they had some involvement, or knew about, the Harper-Givens murders, but there was no substantiation to those rumors.

The common denominator in much of the criminal activity seemed to be Finney Richards.

Finney, of course, was not around to defend himself — but it is perhaps telling that people felt that with Finney six feet under the Warren County soil, they could talk about the crimes.

Whatever Finney's involvement was will likely never be known. Like so much that occurred in that era, the truth was buried along with the key characters.

The saga of Charles Richards, however, was not over.

❖❖❖❖❖

Barbara Flatt first appeared in the *Daily News* in an engagement notice in 1956, announcing the 15-year-old Bowling Green girl was marrying a local man named David Ira Purkerson.

Three years later, Barbara Flatt Purkerson was involved in a violent accident. A traffic light was not working in downtown Bowling Green, leading to a collision between her car and a vehicle being driven by a captain in the city fire department. Purkerson was thrown from the car by the force of the collision and was severely injured.

By 1963, she and David Pukerson had two children, but the marriage was troubled, and Barbara filed for divorce, citing "cruel and inhuman treatment." After the divorce, she was awarded custody of the children.

Her bad luck continued in 1964. She was installing floor tiles in the bathroom of her parents' house when a gallon can of tile glue was placed too close to a gas water heater and ignited. Pukerson tried to leave the room, but a vacuum caused by the flames kept her from being able to open the bathroom door. Her screams drew family members who were able to force open the door, but not before Purkerson's legs were burned. Firefighters soon arrived and extinguished the blaze, but not before causing significant damage to the house.

Four years later, she was in the middle of the Crouse double murders. She was the last one to face a related trial, on charges of obstructing justice based on her changing testimony against Charles Richards.

By fall of 1969, Purkerson was out of jail on the child abandonment charges and living in Louisville. That summer, she had married a man named Roy Lee Wilkins, and the couple were living with Purkerson's sister in the Louisville suburbs.

Her trial was set to start that September in Bowling Green. But as her lawyer was preparing for the trial, he could not get in touch with her.

The day before the trial was to begin, it became clear that Purkerson was missing. When authorities reached out to Purkerson's sister, she confirmed she had recently left town. But she wasn't alone, the sister said. Purkerson had skipped town in the company of none other than Charles Richards.

❖❖❖❖❖

The sister told authorities that Richards had been visiting her house for several weeks looking for Purkerson. He eventually came to the house when she and her husband were there, and after a brief conversation, the trio left without saying a word and hadn't been seen since.

On the day the trial was slated to begin, Purkerson was, not surprisingly, a no-show. A warrant was issued for her arrest and a statewide manhunt began.

Police started receiving tips about her whereabouts, such as that she and her husband were hiding in a trailer near Golden Pond or that she was one of the four people who were found dead recently in a burning car in Tennessee.

Given the violence surrounding the case and the fact that she was last seen with Charles Richards, there was warranted suspicion that Purkerson might never resurface alive.

Police distributed her description to law enforcement agencies across the country — 5-foot-7, 135 pounds with brown hair and blue eyes. Commonwealth Attorney Lowe asked that a federal warrant be issued for her — allowing the search to officially go nationwide.

Several weeks went by with no new leads.

Then in October, police in Vallejo, California, were conducting a roadblock. One of the officers thought he recognized a woman in a car with three others as someone whose photo he had seen on a police wanted bulletin.

She freely admitted she was Barbara Purkerson — now Barbara Wilkins (although for sake of clarity we will continue to call her Barbara Purkerson).

With her in the car were her new husband, Roy Lee Wilkins, her mother Louise Flatt, and — Charles Richards. To make things even more bizarre, Purkerson's mother Louise Flatt told police that she was the wife of Charles Richards — that claim subsequently appeared to be untrue, although they were apparently in a relationship.

Vallejo police contacted the Warren County Sheriff's Office, who confirmed the warrant for Purkerson's arrest and also asked them to hold Richards on pending child endangerment charges, as well on the basis that he was still technically under indictment on the Crouse murder charge.

The pair were taken to the Solano County, California, Jail to await an extradition hearing.

Purkerson waived a challenge to extradition at the hearing in California, and two Warren County sheriff's deputies were dispatched to retrieve her. Richards, however, at first challenged his extradition, but later relented. Sheriff Christy Watts and a deputy then also set out for California to pick him up.

The cost of the effort to return the pair to Warren County was the subject of a front-page article in the *Daily News*, which noted it would cost taxpayers about $2,000 in mileage and per diems.

Whatever the cost, the two were returned to Kentucky uneventfully.

While they awaited trial, Purkerson's lawyer successfully petitioned for a change of venue for the trial because of the local publicity. The trial, slated for early 1970, was moved to Owensboro.

Richards had his day in court first back in Bowling Green. He pleaded guilty to child abandonment and prosecutors suggested a two-year prison sentence. Instead, the judge put Richards on probation so that he could work to pay child support for five years, at which point his children would be 18. He also ordered that Richards be kept in jail until Purkerson's trial was over; it was an unspoken fear that Richards could again disappear with Purkerson.

To satisfy both the work and jail conditions, it was announced that Richards would be working as a cook at the jail.

Purkerson finally was tried in January, but it was anticlimactic. She pleaded guilty to obstructing justice and was given a six-month sentence, with credit for the time served. More newsworthy was that Commonwealth's Attorney Lowe announced he would move to have the murder indictment against Richards dismissed.

And while Richards was off the hook for the Crouse killings, his legal issues were not over. While he worked at the county jail as a cook, Louise Flatt was working as a maid at a local Ramada Inn hotel.

Richards was apparently allowed to leave the jail and allegedly met up with Flatt at the hotel. Using her master key, the pair were accused of entering rooms and stealing items from guests.

The pair were arrested at the hotel and charged with dwellinghouse breaking and accessory to dwellinghouse breaking.

Richards, appearing before a judge, declared "I've been ruined" by the publicity surrounding his indictment in the Crouse case.

"Just make my bond $100,000. I've been ruined anyway," he said.

At their joint trial in May 1970, the pair were convicted of the charges. While they waited for sentencing, the pair officially got married. Any honeymoon would have been brief as the pair were each sentenced to serve 4 years in jail just days later.

After the couple were released from prison, they remained married — and largely out of the spotlight.

So what happened to the Crouses? The fact that Glenn and Leon Miller, who were indicted on charges of robbing the Crouses, were with Finney Richards when Walter Hale was beaten (reportedly for knowing too much), seems likely to be beyond a coincidence.

A theory based on the evidence is that Robert Crouse was recruited, or decided, to come down to Bowling Green because of his demonstrated skill in stealing cars. The car theft business in Bowling Green was starting to take off around that time.

Charles Richards, who once reportedly worked in an auto body shop, also had skills useful for such an operation, and his cousin Finney Richards seemed to have a hand in every criminal enterprise at the time.

As for what went wrong, it could have started with the Millers deciding to relieve the Crouses of some of their cash. After the Crouses left town for a while, they were lured back — perhaps with the promise of protection.

It turned out to be a deadly mistake.

The meeting at Finney Richards' trailer brought together three people with ties to the Crouses — the Miller brothers and the man later accused of killing the Crouses, Charles Richards.

It does not take a stretch of the imagination to consider that Walter Hale was beaten as a warning to not talk about what he knew (whatever that may be) about the Crouse case. Whatever the reality, it will almost certainly stay hidden.

The fate of Dottie Crouse also remains unknown — although there were common rumors that she was adopted by someone in local law enforcement. But with adoption records shielded from public view, the rumor is only that. It is also quite possible that Dottie grew up with a new name — and without ever learning about her unique past.

Chapter 6

LITTLE CHICAGO ERA BEGINS

At the beginning of the 1960s, a young senator from Massachusetts named John F. Kennedy was running a long-shot campaign for the Democratic nomination for president. Vice President Richard Nixon was vying for the Republican nod. Tensions with the Soviet Union, and Cuban leader Fidel Castro, were high; The battle over civil rights was often turning violent, with those advocating for equality becoming frequent targets of bombings, shootings, and beatings.

There were also signs of great progress. The world's first communications satellite, very recently an idea found only in science fiction, was launched. The recent Census showed Bowling Green was the fastest growing city in the state and was now at almost 30,000 residents.

But despite many technological and social advances, life was more like the 1940s and '50s than the turbulent 1960s many imagine when thinking of the decade:

- Newspapers still carried sections titled "news of interest to women" and plenty of pictures of beauty queens.
- Airline stewardesses were required to sign contracts stating that if they got married, they would have to quit their job since they were required, as one article noted, to be "shapely, attractive, poised and charming."
- In August of 1962, more than 10,000 people attended the final day of the Warren County Fair in Bowling Green. The big attraction that day was the crowning of "Miss Southern Kentucky," Freida Friedli. The *Daily News* reported that the 18-year-old "honey blonde … tapes 35-24-36 in the right places."

- Jail inmates in Warren County who misbehaved would be locked in the windowless basement "dungeon" and fed only bread and water.
- There were still so many locals employed in agriculture that a low turnout in a primary election one spring was attributed to a sunny day that had farmers in their fields instead of polling places.

One thing that had remained a constant was the popularity of consuming intoxicating beverages — often procured illegally.

Bootlegging has a long and colorful history across Kentucky. In Bowling Green, Whiskey Run (also spelled Whisky Run) is a natural creek that descends from near Hospital Hill to the Barren River. Its name comes from its use as a water source by bootleggers in the early days of Bowling Green.

Alcohol, both legal and the cheaper, illegal version, was always big business in Bowling Green.

After national Prohibition ended in 1933, many communities across the nation remained "dry," with alcohol sales prohibited. Warren County wasn't one of them.

But in 1957, a group called the Anti-Alcohol Association petitioned to get a local option "wet/dry" question on the ballot. The vote to go dry wasn't close: 4,712 in favor to 2,863 against. The last legal alcoholic drink in Bowling Green was sold on June 21, 1958.

As in the national Prohibition era, criminals seized on the new law and had a field day providing alcohol to the masses, this time without the competition from legal sellers of spirits.

The unintended consequence of the local prohibition effort was to usher in an era of unprecedented crime and violence in Bowling Green.

If one was looking for a symbol to epitomize the era, a stick of dynamite would be an appropriate choice. Dynamite was used to blow up safes, rival businesses — or people. Used in many legitimate ways in farming and construction, dynamite was readily available and very hard to trace.

The number of bombings in Bowling Green increased rapidly starting in 1960.

The year started with news that a trial related to a huge liquor bust would go forward. Walter "June Bug" Simpson managed the private

Amvets Club. He was accused of selling bootleg alcohol out of the establishment, and police had acquired a search warrant. The result was the "biggest Warren County whisky raid since return of prohibition," the *Daily News* reported.

The bust at the Amvets Club also produced other charges that made the case a perfect microcosm of criminal activity at the time; Simpson was also charged with "operating a game of chance."

There were many ways to quench people's thirst to gamble. Various games were offered at roadhouses, bars and even private homes. Pinball machines were also a popular tool as operators would offer cash prizes (as opposed to free turns) to winners of games as an incentive for people to drop their nickels in the slots. It was all illegal.

That February, Bowling Green Police Chief Horace Snell, speaking to the city's civic leaders at a Rotary Club meeting, lamented the fact that police were having trouble enforcing the alcohol law because, he said, people were not forthcoming with information. It was a refrain heard for years to come.

That month, state authorities also raided a local American Legion post where more than 8,000 cans of beer and five slot machines were confiscated. Such raids became common as brewing below the surface of everyday life in the city was a battle — the raids were likely the result of rival liquor operators tipping off police.

"Outgrowth of a large-scale fight for territory between rival bootlegging and gambling interests loom ominously in the background …" The *Daily News* wrote in April 1960.

No one could have predicted how deadly that battle would become over the next decade.

In April, Commonwealth's Attorney Morris Lowe successfully prosecuted Simpson, who was sentenced to 60 days in jail and given a $100 fine. Lowe delivered an ominous warning, saying that if alcohol laws were not vigorously enforced, bootlegging interests could gain control of local government.

Later that month, there was a bizarre public "execution" of the slot machines confiscated at the American Legion. On the banks of the Barren River, Lowe and Warren County Sheriff Joe Hodges took turns smashing the machines with an ax. The metal guts were dumped into the fast-flowing river as an invited newspaper photographer snapped pictures.

But rather than an event that showcased the success of law enforcement, as was intended, it turned out to be an example of the bravado and reach of criminals.

When the photos were developed, someone noticed that one of the originally confiscated new slot machines had been switched for an older, cheaper machine that was destroyed along the riverbank.

Lowe and Hodges began asking questions about the missing machine. A tipster reported that the missing machine could be found behind an Elm tree on the banks of the river. It was found and destroyed. Lowe admitted that evidence had a habit of going missing in Warren County.

Not all the liquor busts were large scale. In May, police descended on the town dump and confiscated 46 cans of beer and a few jugs of home-made "tomato" wine. Two city workers were charged with bootlegging; one claimed to a reporter while he puffed on a cigarette, "I drank a lot but I don't sell any."

One of the police officers was sympathetic as he coughed from the acrid smoke from trash fires.

"You'd have to be drunk to stay out here long," he said.

On the other end of the spectrum, the reportedly largest moonshine operation in the area was busted just days later in Logan County.

Four stills with a combined capacity of 3,000 gallons were found in an old tobacco barn. Two men were arrested. The raid included police from across the region, but was led by legendary federal agent W.B. "Big Six" Henderson.

Although Henderson was a large man, 6-foot-4 and at least 250 pounds, the nickname did not stem from his size, but from the way he hurled a baseball in his semi-pro days. Someone opined that Henderson threw like Hall of Fame pitcher Christy "Big Six" Mathewson, and the name stuck.

Henderson had a reputation as a fearless and relentless chaser of moonshine; he is credited with shutting down about 5,000 stills and sending countless country brewers to jail.

According to some accounts, Henderson was so well known across the state that young girls in Kentucky's "hollers" used his name in jump-rope chants:

"My mother told me ... to watch the still ... in case 'Big Six' ... came over the hill."

Throughout the summer of 1960, raids of clubs, roadhouses and private homes continued regularly as alcohol sales (the going rate for whiskey was $2 a pint) and gambling thrived.

One of the hotspots raided by police was the Silver Slipper nightclub. Behind its green door, equipped with a "prohibition-style" peephole, police found large quantities of beer and wine. While it was primarily an African American establishment, white teenagers and college students also frequented the club, the *Daily News* reported, based on "reliable sources."

Like many other businesses busted then and in years to come, the true owners of the Silver Slipper were hard to determine. The establishments changed hands regularly, and some listed owners were undoubtedly owners in name only.

Despite the city banning alcohol sales, there was a lot of money to be made in the bar and club business, and numerous such establishments opened along Center Street, which soon became known as the "Strip." These "private" clubs were actually open to anyone with cash, regardless of age.

In a front-page article, the *Daily News* reported on the thriving businesses. A photographer and reporter went to an unnamed establishment one afternoon to document the open flow of alcohol. Customers, the paper reported, "were busy celebrating a cocktail hour which lasted all that hot afternoon … they were thirsty and they were willing to pay."

The customers included numerous teenagers … "There are no rules, no regulations — nothing but the whisky and beer flowing out and the money rolling in."

The article noted that time of day did alter the drinking scene: "At night is when things begin to rock in Bowling Green speakeasies — the time when suckers pay homage to the games of chance and the time when pistol-packing patrons decide to settle differences Wild West style."

One estimate from the time was that there were 350, or more, people involved in the illegal alcohol business in Bowling Green. While there was of course the risk of arrest, the typical fines were a drop in the bucket compared to the gush of moonshine cash.

All that summer, there were almost daily raids targeting liquor sales. Most involved small, home-based operators, but the occasional "big fish" was reeled in as when police raided the Riverside Club and found a trap door hiding cases of whiskey.

As the raids started to lead to bootlegging convictions (a typical sentence was 30 days of "hard labor" in jail and a $100 fine), city prosecutor Joe C. Covington joined the chorus warning that Bowling Green was facing a "dangerous cancer" of lawlessness.

He told a jury in a bootlegging case that "you must decide whether (the city) will be a good place to live and raise your children, or let a bunch of bootleggers take it over. … I doubt if you realize how close your city is to being taken over by bootleggers."

He later added that it was clear that many of the people being arrested on bootlegging charges were just the frontline workers for those running illegal activity behind the scenes.

Those individuals were also using police to take out competitors.

In late June, a "plush" new Amvets club was raided, leading to the confiscation of some hard liquor and about 700 bottles of beer. Like the American Legion bust earlier in the year, the person who told police about the operation was likely linked to rival liquor peddlers. The Amvets club president said frankly, "It couldn't be any other way."

The bootleggers were also using every trick in the book to avoid police — rather than store alcohol in easily searched buildings, it'd be stashed in adjoining bushes or cars, to be fetched upon order. They would also switch house address numbers daily; police arriving with a search warrant would often find themselves at the right house, but with faulty paperwork.

At this point, overt violence between rival bootleggers was still rare; although there were persistent rumors that Bowling Green's own version of the Chicago mob's St. Valentine's Day massacre was narrowly averted. Two groups of heavily armed bootleggers had apparently run into each other on a country road outside of town; bloodshed was averted when one of the groups beat a hasty retreat.

Meanwhile, in response to a petition circulating around the city to call for a new referendum on alcohol sales, the Warren County Anti-Liquor Association opened an office in downtown Bowling Green. The bootleggers who were cashing in on the illicit liquor trade were undoubtedly cheering the group on.

The *Daily News* published an editorial in July noting that drunk-driving cases had soared since local prohibition, further evidence, the editorial stated, of "another clear indication of prohibition's failure."

That same month, a group calling itself "The Citizen's Committee for Law and Order," filed a petition with 7,011 signatures seeking a September vote on the city's alcohol ban. Attorney G.D. Milliken Jr., speaking on behalf of the group, said the issue wasn't about alcohol, but the current system where "bootleggers and gangsters are getting rich, tax-free."

The head of the Warren County Anti-Liquor Association, a local Baptist church pastor, said his group's poll of local residents showed 69 percent against legal alcohol.

In the leadup to the vote, the Anti-Liquor Association confirmed it would be bringing in out-of-town "detectives" (essentially security guards) to help ensure a fair vote.

The day before the referendum, the *Daily News* published a rare front-page editorial, calling prohibition a failure and urging residents to vote "yes" on "law and order."

On election day, massive lines formed at the polling locations across the city. Prohibitionists wore "No" buttons and passed out yellow cards asking people to "pray before you vote." The referendum supporters wore "yes" buttons, making the sides easy to discern. There were some verbal skirmishes, but no violence.

A total of 10,590 votes — a number that surpassed the previous record total when the city went dry in 1957 — were cast. This time the wet vote prevailed easily, 6,670 to 3,920.

Those who believed, and successfully argued, that the end of prohibition meant the end to the rise of illegal activity in the city were incredibly mistaken, as they were about to find out. Just days after the liquor vote, the *Daily News* reported that local law enforcement "generally agreed that the return of legal sales will automatically eliminate nearly all bootleggers operating in the city … ."

They were grossly mistaken. It seemed neither prohibition nor legal alcohol sales was the answer to the crime wave. In less than a year after the 1960 vote, there were nine reported bombing attempts in the city.

The "wet" vote had left the city an oasis of legally obtained alcohol in a desert of surrounding dry counties. Soon, unscrupulous bar and liquor storeowners were battling with bootleggers to be the primary providers of alcohol for the entire region.

Adjacent to some of the bars and liquor stores would be a warehouse where cases of liquor would be sold out the back door to individuals who would then take it to the "dry" areas to resell at a hefty markup. The hands of Bowling Green police were tied because their jurisdiction ended at the city limits.

One Bowling Green police officer later recalled seeing cars leaving the establishments "so loaded down with half pints they'd almost burst their springs."

"A lot of places would actually have delivery services," he said. The buyers in outlying counties "wanted a schedule. They wanted (the alcohol) delivered at 4 a.m., before the local sheriff woke up."

The illicit liquor business in Bowling Green was largely divided into two factions: a north side squad that sold to northern areas, including Butler, Barren and Edmonson counties, while the southside group mostly sold to points south – Logan, Simpson and Allen counties.

As city residents awaited the formal end of prohibition at the end of the year, crowds nearly equaling those seen in the recent referendum descended on downtown Bowling Green in October to see the Democratic nominee for president speak on a platform outside City Hall. Thousands mobbed Senator Kennedy as he told attendees the best "two-horse parlay in Kentucky (was) Western Kentucky State College's basketball team in the winter and the Democratic Party, winter and summer."

Bowling Green Mayor R.D. Graham presented Kennedy with a country ham, which the Massachusetts senator promised to eat.

Two weeks later, two massive explosions rocked Bowling Green in a span of five hours.

A bomb shattered the silence of a quiet neighborhood when it exploded from underneath a station wagon around midnight. No one was injured. The car belonged to city council member Geroge Dillard. Dillard was, not surprisingly given his occupation as a wholesale liquor salesman, a proponent of ending prohibition in the city in the recent vote.

A few hours later, several sticks of dynamite placed in an air conditioner exploded in the office of the Siddens Music Company. Owner Bill Siddens was sleeping nearby but escaped uninjured, despite the massive destruction from the explosion that saw inch-thick pieces of wood embedded in concrete block walls.

Siddens said it was clear that the bomb "was meant to be a killing — a final exit for me."

Several people, including a Bowling Green police officer, had seen a man driving a 1954 sedan around the latter blast scene. Police quickly found the car in front of a nearby home. When they entered the home, they found an Edmonson County man named Billy H. Graham, 31, in bed, but fully clothed.

Graham, who had a long criminal history and was working as a house painter, was arrested.

Most believed the blasts were related, with bootleggers the likely culprit.

"New York doesn't seem to have anything on Bowling Green and we don't like it when we start getting more than our share of bombings," Commonwealth's Attorney Lowe said.

A few days later, Graham appeared in court for a preliminary hearing. His own 9-year-old son was the star witness against his father, telling the court he saw a "whole bunch" of items in his father's car, with the elder Graham reportedly telling his son he needed to be careful because some of it was dynamite.

Siddens also testified that he had received numerous death threats, but it was unclear in the court testimony why.

Graham, nervously puffing on cigarettes during the hearing, didn't testify.

The next month, prohibition in Bowling Green ended quietly — thanks in part to the "bootleggers' wireless."

Police decided to make one more round of alcohol busts on Nov. 25, a Friday night. But the bootleggers got word of the plan, and undercover police were only able to find one pint of whiskey for sale.

It was a different story a month later when four soldiers from nearby Fort Campbell came to Bowling Green for some drinks. The result was a brawl with the four soldiers beaten and stabbed by some local men at the Amvets Club. Police investigating the brawl found gambling devices and plenty of alcohol.

Later in December, the city's new alcohol control board started accepting the dozens of applications for liquor licenses in the city. There was no doubt that there was money to be made selling liquor — illegally and legitimately. The problem for the bootleggers was that, even if they were interested in going straight, the state limited Bowling

Green to 18 retail liquor licenses (there were unlimited licenses available for pool halls and other establishments serving only beer).

By December, 48 applications had already been filed for liquor licenses. Those left out had two options — find a new business venture, or sell alcohol illegally, as they had already been doing.

The first day of (once again) legal alcohol sales in the city was February 15, 1961.

Two police officers were on a routine patrol on Boatlanding Road that night when they noticed an unusual package next to the Last Chance Liquor Store building. Upon closer inspection, they realized it was a bundle of dynamite. The long fuse had burned out before igniting the bomb, but police estimated the bundle of 29 sticks would have not only blown up the liquor store, with its owners asleep inside, but also shaken the entire northern half of Bowling Green.

The store owner was a city constable, Roy "Toots" Cline, and his wife. While Toots Cline declined to speculate on the reason for the attempted bombing, it was no secret that he was one of the grassroots leaders of the effort to end prohibition.

The bombings kept coming. In April, more than 300 sticks of dynamite were stolen from a Bowling Green quarry. The next night, the 31-W Lunch Room (despite the name, it was more of a tavern) was blasted by 20 or more sticks of dynamite. The explosion shattered windows at several nearby businesses, but no one was injured.

The news of the bombings continued to make headlines in local papers, but soon shared space with stories about a situation in Newport involving the Cleveland mob, a former NFL player turned reform politician and a long-legged stripper who went by the name April Flowers.

Chapter 7

KENTUCKY'S SIN CITY

Newport, Kentucky, seems an unlikely place to become a haven for criminal activity. Tucked into the remote northeastern corner of the state, it would likely have never grown much if not for the fact that it sat on a fortuitous spot on the Ohio River — directly across from Cincinnati.

As that city grew, so did Newport - not quite a suburb but tied to the city in many ways. As industry and river traffic grew, so did the city's population. By 1900, Newport was the state's third most populous city.

As in many other cities, Prohibition proved to be the catalyst for the rise of organized crime. But what set Newport apart - for decades to come - was how extensive, brazen and resilient organized crime became in the city, which became one of the handful of "open cities" in the country where any vice could be openly indulged.

❖❖❖❖❖

From its earliest days, Newport was a haven for those seeking to break the law, or who were looking to elude law enforcement. The isolated little town, largely cut off to the north and east by the Ohio River and the west by the Licking River, was once commonly known as "Little Mexico."

But growth came steadily, and even before Prohibition, Newport was the place to go to indulge in various vices, with gambling the big moneymaker. Seeing an opportunity, enterprising criminals set up shop in Newport knowing that they would have a steady flow of customers and seeing that local authorities were mostly concerned about filling their pockets with bribe money.

Soon Newport was filled with bars, gambling dens and brothels; with plenty of neon signs on the main drag, Monmouth Street, acting as beacons for those looking for a drink, a bet, or female companionship.

The clubs, some as posh as found in any big city, hosted a slew of famous performers — everyone from B.B. King to Miles Davis and Aretha Franklin – but vice was the biggest business in town, leading to Newport earning the nickname "Sin City."

The city soon drew the attention of national crime figures. Most noteworthy, a criminal syndicate known as the Cleveland Four was behind many of the illicit businesses in Newport. Named for the four men with Cleveland ties who ran the syndicate, the Cleveland Four were experts at bootlegging, with Newport a key hub for the distribution of illegal alcohol.

Prostitution was also big business in Newport, with many customers coming from across the river in Cincinnati, which, a 1961 Time magazine article noted, was just a $1.35 cab ride away. One enterprising brothel owner pioneered a way to make even more money from the sex trade. He rigged his brothel rooms with audio recorders. The women workers were encouraged to get their customers to discuss their home life before getting down to "business." The brothel owner would then confront the men with the recording, offering to destroy the tapes in exchange for a few thousand dollars.

The *Time* magazine article reported that a local had tracked the goings-on at one popular local brothel and found that during the busiest times, the 11 women working there averaged a new customer every seven minutes.

Eventually, there were calls for a crackdown on criminal activity. There were various efforts, at the local, state and even national levels, to clean up Newport since the early 1900s. But the efforts were no match for the money, influence and violent tactics of the city's criminal kingpins, who often were allied with national criminal syndicates.

A 1957 article in *Esquire* magazine outlined the criminal enterprise that was Newport, estimating that a million visitors came to Newport each year to indulge in criminal activity, producing a $30 million windfall. Of that, an estimated $1 million was used for bribes and kickbacks. Aside from bribes, the criminal element in Newport never shied away from using violence to stay in business.

Further complicating reform efforts was the fact that many legitimate businesses depended on the revenue from the visitors to stay afloat. Even if many residents did not endorse the illegal activity, their livelihood depended on it.

But by 1960, the calls for reform started to gradually become louder than the calls for the status quo.

Groups like Newport's Ministerial Association asked the governor to remove corrupt officials and began public campaigns for reform.

The effort to clean up Newport soon garnered a prominent local figurehead.

George Ratterman, 34, was a regional hero. The gridiron star from Cincinnati played four sports at Notre Dame, including as a quarterback on the football team. He then played professional football for nine years. He led the NFL in touchdown passes in 1950 and was featured on the cover of *Sports Illustrated*.

When his career ended in 1956, he moved to the wealthy enclave of Fort Thomas, Kentucky. Fort Thomas is in Campbell County, where Newport is also located. Ratterman had earned a law degree and aside from serving as legal counsel for a business in Cincinnati and working for ABC as a commentator on NFL games, he was running a local youth football league in 1961 when he was approached by representatives of a new group called the Committee of 500.

The group was formed with a goal to bolster the efforts to end Newport's cycle of corruption and had the backing of many of the county's wealthier citizens. Ratterman was part of the group and agreed to run for Campbell County sheriff.

The incumbent sheriff, Norbert Roll, had announced he would not seek reelection. He had been recently indicted on charges of "nonfeasance." Even though he was eventually acquitted, he decided to hang up his badge.

Hundreds of county residents attended a rally at a local library in April to hear from Ratterman, who drew a standing ovation.

Ratterman said his candidacy was "a fight of morality against filth, of right against wrong."

He said his family — he and his wife had eight children — had already started receiving threats that one of his children could be "accidently" run over because of his candidacy, and he knew many people were doubtful that real reform was possible after decades of corruption.

"I don't want (my children) to grow up in a community where syndicated gambling finds a home, where prostitution flourishes, where officials are known to be corrupt, where alcohol is sold to minors at all hours of the day and night and where … the illegal narcotics industry has also found a home. I don't want my children to grow up in such a community, and I don't intend to move. There is only one answer — do everything I can to help clean up Campbell County."

He also told the adoring crowd that he anticipated many personal attacks in the weeks ahead.

Notably, one of the attendees at the rally — reportedly the only one who did not join in the applause for Ratterman — was a man named Albert "Red" Masterson. Along with "Red," Masterson had another nickname — "The Enforcer" — for his well-known exploits in protecting his illicit businesses. Masterson at one point was head of the crime syndicate-backed Newport Civic Association, which had a slogan of "Clean Up, Not Close Up" – another way of saying leave things as they are.

When a reporter asked Masterson if Ratterman had a chance to "clean up" Newport after repeated failed attempts, Masterson responded, "I am still waiting to see it."

But the state's largest newspaper, The *Louisville Courier-Journal*, noted in an editorial that Ratterman could succeed where others failed.

The paper noted that some previous reform candidates had developed a case of "Newport Eye. A rare disease that makes public officials unable to see prostitution, gambling or other law-breaking."

As for Ratterman, "No one who knows him believes that … he can or will be bribed or intimidated by the mobsters and hoodlums who run the gambling dens and brothels of Newport … ," the paper wrote.

His opponents started calling Ratterman the "second-stringer" — a reference to the fact that he often sat on the bench behind other quarterbacks in his football career.

G.W. "Hoot" Gibson was running for sheriff on the Democratic ticket. Gibson made it clear what side he was on when he told a reporter, "I've never seen any" vice in Newport.

But it was clear that the criminal element was worried about Ratterman's candidacy, as well as the possibility the state would step in amid increasing pressure.

One source told a reporter that the criminals had been advised to "lay low" for a while.

But it soon became clear that they had no intention of doing so.

In late April, a car bomb seriously injured a local woman who was a leader in the Committee of 500, and the Ratterman home became the frequent target of harassing phone calls.

But the gridiron star started racking up more endorsements for his candidacy from local religious and other civic groups. It was clear that he was on a potential path to victory.

Then came the bombshell.

While the details of what happened would come to be disputed, this much is certain. Ratterman, in the company of a local strip-tease dancer known as April Flowers, was arrested at a Newport hotel and charged with breach of peace, disorderly conduct and resisting arrest. Flowers was charged with prostitution.

Not surprisingly, the development led to banner headlines in state and national newspapers.

According to Newport police, they received an anonymous call around 2:30 a.m. May 9, saying someone was engaged in prostitution at the Glenn Hotel. The hotel was in the same building as the Tropicana nightclub where the 26-year-old Flowers (real name Juanita Jean Hodges, of Houston, Texas) was a featured strip-tease dancer.

Three detectives entered the building where they encountered a former college football star named Tito Carinci. Carinci was managing the Tropicana and tried to stop the detectives from entering, they claimed. They arrested him on charges of breach of the peace and proceeded to the hotel suite. Upon entering, they said they found Ratterman in bed with Flowers, wearing only a shirt and his socks. Flowers was in a robe hiked up around her waist.

According to detectives, Ratterman jumped from the bed and pushed one of them. He was arrested and taken to the jail with a bedspread wrapped around his waist.

Ratterman eventually posted a $500 bond and was released.

Through a spokesman — one of the leaders of the Committee of 500 — Ratterman claimed he had been framed. According to his account, he had gotten a call from an "old friend" asking him to come to a Cincinnati hotel for a drink. He did, and they were later joined by another friend. Ratterman said he must have been drugged and taken to the Glenn Hotel. Flowers was already in the room, he claimed, with police arriving a short time later.

To prove his innocence, after he was released from jail, Ratterman went to a local hospital to get his blood drawn to show he had been drugged.

Later that day, Ratterman held a press conference at his home to detail further what he said happened.

Ratterman said he had been trying to convince Carinci, an old football acquaintance, to give up his job at the Tropicana. A mutual friend, an Ohio businessman named Thomas Paisley, called Ratterman to say Carinci wanted to meet with him. The three then met at a Cincinnati hotel and had some drinks.

Carinci then invited the others to come back to Newport and have dinner in his suite at the Glenn Hotel.

Ratterman said he at first declined.

"I mentioned again I did not believe his place of business was a proper one in which I should be seen," he said.

But eventually, against Ratterman's better judgement, the three men went to Carinci's hotel suite for steak dinners and some drinks.

"Shortly thereafter, I suddenly became quite groggy and stretched out on a bed in the bedroom," Ratterman said. "I recall nothing more until I was awakened by the commotion."

The "commotion," he said, was the police officers "tearing at my shirt and trousers."

He said they tore off his pants and pushed him to the ground.

"I was so groggy and weak I could hardly lift my arms," he said.

He said he passed out, and when he came to, Flowers was in the room.

"I have no idea who she was and never have seen her before," Ratterman claimed.

He said his blood test from that morning showed he had chloral hydrate — a sedative referred to on the streets as "knockout drops" — in his system — proof that he had been drugged and framed.

He also showed his torn pants.

Reporters asked Ratterman if he believed Carinci was part of the effort to frame him.

"It could have been several persons," he said. "I think I was indiscreet in where I went and I won't be so naive after this."

As for Mrs. Ratterman, she told reporters she was "mad" — but not at her husband.

"I was not 100 percent behind George's campaign at the beginning, but I am now," Anne Ratterman said. (Her reluctance was not just based on fear but the fact that the position paid a paltry $7,200 a year — a 50 percent pay cut from his current salary.)

Her husband said he would continue his run for office.

In light of Ratterman's claim of police misconduct, Newport Mayor Ralph Mussman announced he had opened an investigation into the police department — led by two Newport police officials. The FBI had also reportedly started investigating the case, as was a local grand jury.

One of the police detectives at the Glenn Hotel the night of the arrest, Pat Ciarfardini, was coming under special scrutiny. Ciarfardini was off duty that night, so it was unclear why he was there. When a reporter questioned him, he went to great lengths to explain he was at a Fraternal Order of Police meeting in Bowling Green most of that day and night — only returning to Newport in time to hear about the prostitution claim and deciding to tag along.

As the probes continued, it appeared that the biggest impact was to bolster the reform efforts. In the 48 hours after the arrest, the Committee of 500 claimed more than 500 additional people joined the organization.

A *Louisville Courier-Journal* reporter who visited Newport wrote that the crime bosses were again looking to lay low, acknowledging that the Ratterman arrest had galvanized the reform movement.

"The alleged attempt to frame Ratterman has backfired so completely, according to many observers, that the gamblers may close down until after the November elections," he wrote.

On May 16, the trial of Ratterman, Flowers and Carinci was slated to begin, with Newport's special counselor (akin to a city attorney), Thomas Hirschfield, acting as prosecutor.

The proceedings had to be moved to a larger courtroom because of the interest. Court officials and police had their hands full that morning trying to keep the massive crowds who wanted to attend the trial in order. Newspaper, radio and TV reporters from across the country were also on hand.

The presiding judge ruled that the charges against Flowers would be heard first.

The two tables with the defendants offered a stark visual contrast – Ratterman sat next to his faithful wife; the mother of their eight children; Carinci sat between two young and attractive Tropicana dancers — Flowers and Rita Desmond (whose real name was Bonnie Green, a 22-year-old Texas native), who was also apparently part of the night's events.

Newport detectives started by testifying about the arrest, largely restating the official version of events. A detective testified that

Ratterman had shown no signs of impairment to indicate he had been drugged. Another testified Carinci was crying after being arrested, and he heard Ratterman say, "Don't cry Tito. It was just one of those things that happened. We just got nailed, that's all."

Carinci also testified to his version of events that night.

He said after some drinking in Cincinnati with Paisley and Ratterman, Paisley was aggressively demanding that "they go across the river to Newport and get some girls."

He eventually agreed. After going to the Glenn Hotel and entering via a back door to avoid being seen, Carinci said he decided to invite two Tropicana dancers, Flowers and Desmond, to go up to his suite and "have a drink with a couple friends of mine."

Since Flowers was currently on stage, Carinci said he motioned to the house band to cut her act short.

He said he later saw Ratterman "kissing" and hugging Flowers (he described Ratterman as having a "Valentino grip" on the dancer) while Paisley and Desmond left the suite together.

He denied that he was intending for the women to do anything other than have a drink with the two men.

Carinci said he would be willing to take a lie-detector test to prove his version of events was true. He added that he had gone to church that morning "and I knelt before an altar and swore my statement was true. George, could you do it," he said, looking at Ratterman.

Paisley, meanwhile, testified that much of the night was a blur — not because he had drank too much but, presumably, because he also had been drugged at some point.

He said what drew him to cross the river to Newport that night was steak, not sex. We were "going over there only for steaks," he said.

Ratterman also testified saying his memory of the night was like "blurred snapshots." He again recounted a "commotion" in the room and someone pulling off his pants, although he now testified he could not remember who.

He said he remembered a woman in red being in the hotel room, but didn't recognize Flowers until he saw her picture in the newspaper the next day.

Ratterman testified that he believed Carinci, or someone under his direction, had drugged his drink.

After the end of the testimony, the prosecutor asked that the charges against Flowers be reduced to breach of the peace, likely because there had been no testimony to indicate that Flowers had been paid for sex, or that there had been any sexual conduct.

The judge deferred on issuing a verdict on the charges against Flowers, and the next day, huge crowds again descended on the courthouse as the case against Ratterman was heard.

Ratterman's defense attorney, Henry Cook, homed in on the assertion that Ratterman was framed. In a heated exchange with the prosecutor, Cook said the plot against his client was hatched as soon as he announced his candidacy.

As with the Flowers trial, Newport detectives were the first to testify.

Under cross examination by Cook, Ciarfardini said that Ratterman appeared to him to have been drunk the night of his arrest. While that could explain Ratterman's apparent memory loss, that directly contradicted the other detectives who said Ratterman appeared normal.

Cook also hammered Ciarfardini on his knowledge of the criminal activity at the Tropicana/Glenn Hotel.

Ciarfardini said he knew the facility as only "a lounge."

The judge (and public) also got to hear for the first time from the Tropicana dancers in the Ratterman trial.

Desmond said Ratterman and Paisley were at first "bashful" when she met them in Carinci's suite. But she said things eventually heated up after Flowers arrived, with Paisley asking to go to her room "for a drink" because Ratterman and Flowers wanted to be alone.

Desmond said Paisley then "tried to make love to me in my room, but didn't succeed." She said Paisley offered her $50 to go with him to his Cincinnati hotel room, but she declined.

Flowers said when she entered the suite, Ratterman was sitting on a bed. She said Ratterman gave her a pen with his name on it as a "souvenir." He then went into the bathroom. That was when, Flowers said, she went into another room of the suite and took off her bra and G-string, part of her dancing "slave" costume, because it was uncomfortable, but she still had on a robe.

She went back into the bedroom and Ratterman was back on the bed, but now only wearing his shirt and socks.

"However, I must say his shirt was pretty long, so it wasn't too embarrassing," she said.

She sat on the bed and "he tried to embrace me," she said.

At that point, police stormed into the room, she testified.

Flowers said she had no idea who Ratterman was, other than Carinci introducing him and Paisley as good friends of his.

Ratterman then again testified to his belief that he had been drugged, and his recollection of events was hazy. He reiterated that he expected such attacks because of his reform candidacy.

He added that he had not spoken to Carinci for about two years before he was contacted through Paisley about the three men meeting. He also said he would be willing to submit to a lie-detector test to prove his version of events.

Ratterman's doctor then testified about taking a blood sample that morning from Ratterman. The sample was sent to a lab for analysis. A Cincinnati doctor who analyzed the sample said he found chloral hydrate in Ratterman's blood.

The prosecutor argued that the tubes containing Ratterman's blood sample could have been contaminated.

Carinci, sitting at a separate defense table from Ratterman with Flowers and Desmond at his side, often appeared bored by the testimony. A newspaper photographer captured an image of the burly ex-football player blowing bubble gum.

Newport's Mayor, Ralph Mussman, also downplayed the trial. When asked about the national press that descended on Newport to cover the trial, he said the case was nothing more than "a $10 Police Court Case blown up out of proportion."

Showing more interest in the case and the general lawlessness in Newport was U.S. Attorney General Robert F. Kennedy, brother of President John F. Kennedy. Ratterman and RFK had a mutual friend — a Cincinnati attorney named William Geoghan, who apparently served as a go-between for the two men.

During testimony that week to a committee of the House, which was considering stronger organized crime laws, Robert Kennedy used Newport as an example of a place where organized crime was rampant.

"There is wide-open gambling in Newport … ," Kennedy said, adding that there was evidence that casino profits were going to at least 11 individuals who lived outside the state.

The case also made national news on the same day as the Ratterman trial began when it was revealed that a federal grand jury, at Kennedy's behest, had opened a probe into the situation.

The trial adjourned for the day amid continuing testimony from various doctors regarding the blood samples.

The next morning, the prosecutor got a doctor to admit that there was no way to tell when the chloral hydrate had entered Ratterman's bloodstream.

Ratterman then took the stand and again recounted a night that grew into a hazy blur after having a single scotch and soda at the Glenn.

Prosecutor Hirschfield asked Ratterman, who admitted he had been at the Tropicana on numerous occasions before, why he had taken no action to report the illegal activity there.

He replied that there seemed no reason to, given the generally accepted acknowledgement that the Newport police would not do anything. He added that he had done as much as anyone else, including Hirschfield.

"How do you know I haven't done anything?" the prosecutor asked.

"Because (the conditions) still exist," Ratterman replied to laughter.

The trial adjourned for the day with an unusual Saturday session scheduled.

That day, what was already a sensational case was hit with a proverbial bomb that, as one newspaper reported, "Rocks Newports' Vice Empire."

❖❖❖❖❖

Taking the stand for Ratterman's defense was a mild-mannered local photographer named Thomas Withrow.

Withrow testified that he had been called in April by a local attorney named Charles Lester, who happened to be the lawyer representing Carinci and Flowers, about taking some photos.

Withrow said Lester told him to go to the Glenn Hotel and see a man named "Marty." He did, and Marty told him to be ready to take a picture of a man and a woman at the hotel at a date to be determined.

"They'll be in a room. We'll open the door, you take the picture, and we'll jump out," Withrow claimed Marty told him.

Despite a promise that he would be well-paid and "protected," Withrow said he had no intention of taking the photo as the need for "protection" made him wary.

"I was going to wash my hands of the whole cotton-pickin' works," he said.

Withrow's wife then testified that someone called their house around 1:30 a.m. May 9, the day of the Ratterman arrest, looking for her husband. When she said he wasn't home, the man left a message asking him to call "Marty at the Glenn Hotel."

The phone continued to ring periodically until the calls stopped about 3 a.m. — the time of Ratterman's arrest.

"Marty" had provided a phone number to Withrow, which was traced back to a man named Edward Anthony Buccieri. In discussing the goings-on at the Tropicana, police had previously testified that Buccieri was one of the operators of the Tropicana — and was commonly called Marty. (Later reached by reporters, Buccieri declined comment.)

In light of the stunning testimony supporting the claim that Ratterman was being framed, prosecutor Hirschfield asked the judge to dismiss the charges.

"I think this should be presented to a grand jury," he said, adding that he knew Withrow and believed him.

The judge agreed and dismissed the charges against Ratterman.

But the bombshell testimony would likely never have happened if it weren't for a persistent grandmother.

After Ratterman's arrest, Withrow decided to keep quiet about what he knew — for the most part.

Ratterman's attorney Henry Cook relayed the series of events that led to the shocking testimony.

Withrow was at the local hospital to take some pictures, coincidentally at the same time that Ratterman was there to give a blood sample. The photographer had been overheard by a nurse saying he had almost gotten mixed up in the case.

The nurse told Ratterman's doctor, who was also on the Committee of 500, about what she heard. The doctor in turn relayed the information to Cook.

Cook then met with the Withrows and Nancy Hay, 68, who was the grandmother of the photographer's wife and knew about the situation.

At first, the Withrows were adamant they would not testify, out of fear for their safety.

Hay, however, later called Cook and told him she had known his father, who had been Newport's police chief for 47 years. She said she would testify as to what she knew out of a sense of civic duty. The Withrows then agreed that they would also testify.

Cook also told reporters that as many as 100 people - mostly members of the Committee of 550 — knew about Withrow's testimony but managed to keep it quiet.

Many attended the trial and rushed to shake Ratterman's hand after the dismissal; some burst out in tears. As Ratterman, his wife and lawyer made their way out of the courtroom, his supporters sent him off with a standing ovation.

"I consider it full vindication," Ratterman told reporters. "I'm very happy the trial is over."

The next day, more than 500 people attended a Committee of 500 rally to hear from Ratterman and his supporters.

"We knew how the trial would end," Ratterman said. "But it was still distasteful to my family and friends to sit through five days of slander. This is not a political fight, but a moral one, and we will win because God is on our side."

Days later, Ratterman publicly called on Gov. Bert Combs to get state police involved in tackling Newport vice — a familiar request but one that had a renewed sense of urgency with the November election looming.

The next day, Combs told reporters he believed Ratterman had been framed, and he was considering action, but that he didn't want to "telegraph my punches."

Meanwhile, the results of the grand jury probe into the case were expected to be released May 25.

That day, in a banner headline the Kentucky Post newspaper reported "COUNTY TENSE AWAITING JURY'S REPORT ON 'RAID'".

And like so much in this case, the grand jury probe yielded a surprise.

Two people were indicted on charges of conspiring to bring a false prosecution of Ratterman: Carinci, as expected, and his old "friend" — Paisley.

Newspapers and national publications like *Time* and *Look* magazines speculated that the developments could spell — finally — a real crackdown on vice in Newport. Adding to the momentum, Gov. Combs appointed a special prosecutor to look into the situation, and even publicly called out local Newport officials for turning a blind eye to the corruption.

Some local vice establishments temporarily closed their doors, but there was still broad skepticism that real change was afoot. One local told a newspaper reporter he believed Ratterman would be elected sheriff if the election were held then – but November was still five months away, and Newport's crime lords were not going to give up their lucrative business easily.

In early June, a federal grand jury was also slated to hear testimony in the Ratterman case. Flowers was one of the called witnesses. As she waited to be called to testify in a federal courtroom, a newspaper photographer snapped several pictures of the dancer, who now sported blonde hair rather than her natural brunette locks. In one picture, she holds up her 1960 Kentucky Colonel commission – even though being named a Kentucky Colonel was only honorary, that she had gotten the honor indicated she had some friends or admirers in high places (rumors were that the person who sponsored Flowers for the honor was a prominent local judge).

It turned out Flowers never testified that day — the local U.S. Attorney General announced he was putting the grand jury probe on hold for at least several months, for undisclosed reasons.

But the grand jury had a mind of its own, and announced it would be investigating the Ratterman case immediately. A long list of witnesses began testifying behind closed doors to the federal grand jury.

Meanwhile, the trial of Carinci and Paisley began June 19. Ratterman was the star witness for the prosecutors. After again laying out his version of events, he was aggressively cross examined by the defense lawyers. They hammered him on inconsistencies in his accounts and that of others — there was testimony for example that Ratterman, Carinci and Paisley had made another stop at a lounge in Cincinnati before heading to Newport, and Ratterman had given various accounts of whether he had anything to eat that night.

Ratterman again stated that much of the night was a blur, and he said outright he did not believe Paisley was involved in the drugging.

Defense attorneys hammered on the testimony that Ratterman (and Paisley) were looking for some female companionship that night.

"No, that is not true sir," Ratterman responded.

"Well, you ended up with (a woman), didn't you," the attorney asked.

"Unfortunately," Ratterman said.

Defense attorneys also cast doubt on the finding of drugs in Ratterman's system. The candidate's doctor testified that it was Ratterman's cousin, James Knecht, who first contacted him about taking a blood sample from Ratterman. Knecht worked for a pharmaceutical company and, the doctor admitted, could have had access to the drugs found in Ratterman's system.

The prosecution rested, with the defense then slated to present their case.

It turns out they didn't need to.

The case against both men was legally joined, meaning both had to be found guilty or both innocent.

The judge shocked most observers during the trial by directing the jury to deliver a not-guilty verdict.

"There is not one iota of evidence to establish any conspiracy between these two men," the judge said.

Ratterman said after the surprise verdict that he was happy his friend Paisley was vindicated. He did not mention Carinci.

The federal grand jury probe, meanwhile, continued in secret. But the pressure was on as AG Kennedy again pointed to Newport as the gambling capitol of the entire southern region of the country. A federal grand jury in New Orleans returned indictments on several Newport gambling figures that week, and Gov. Combs announced he had enlisted some experts for advice on how to eradicate vice in a community.

The governor was also moving ahead on proceedings to remove four Campbell County officials — Sheriff Norbert Roll, Newport police department Chief George Gugel and Chief of Detectives LeRoy Fredericks and county Chief of Police Harry Stuart.

Amid the flurry of activity, several of the Newport clubs closed their doors and others, like the Tropicana, saw a sharp decline in business.

And to add insult to injury, Flowers' Kentucky Colonel designation was rescinded.

The removal procedures against the four men featured a slew of testimony from those involved in the Newport underworld, including a former prostitute and madam, Vivian Schulte, who recounted providing envelopes with between $50 and $100 every Monday to various officials, including Gugel, Fredericks and Newport detective Ciarfardini. She also implicated local judges, prosecutors, including local Commonwealth's Attorney William Wise, and others in law enforcement in the payoffs.

Wise, the *Courier-Journal* noted in an article, had once called the Ministerial Association "A group of little men from little churches trying to make a name for themselves."

Now, Wise was under investigation and a prominent judge named by Schulte as getting payoffs recused himself from any related proceedings.

Not surprisingly, the federal grand jury indicated it was also interested in hearing from Schulte. The grand jury finally announced three indictments, but none directly related to Ratterman. Three men were charged with perjury for lying to the grand jury about their involvement in the prostitution business in Newport.

While the federal grand jury probe and removal proceedings seemed to bog down, a local grand jury stepped in and issued indictments against a who's who of Newport officials claiming they engaged in a conspiracy to obstruct justice.

Those indicted included Mayor Ralph Mussman, the city manager, three of the four city commissioners and numerous current and former members of the police department, including Gugel, Fredericks and Ciarfardini. A slew of resignations followed.

A newspaper headline summed up the developments in a story headlined "Newport Vice Empire Caving … "

Many gambling and prostitution operators began closing up shop permanently.

After a half century of failed efforts to clean up the wide-open town, the noose was tightening on Newport vice. In October, Governor Combs signed an order that banned Gugel and Fredericks from holding public office — he couldn't remove them from their jobs because they had both "retired."

In a last-ditch effort to preserve what they could of the Newport status quo, a group calling itself the City Businessmen and Taxpayers League was formed. It claimed the Committee of 500 was ruining Newport business and put up its own slate of candidates.

On the eve of the election, Flowers was in the news once again. In an interview with the *Courier-Journal*, she said she was an unwitting pawn in the effort to frame Ratterman and was cooperating with the FBI in an investigation. She admitted that when she first saw Ratterman at the hotel suite, he was already passed out on the bed and was fully clothed.

She tried to wake him up, but he only managed a mumble before police burst into the room. She recognized Ciarfardini, she said, and left the room. When she heard a commotion "like fighting," she returned and asked Ciarfardini what was happening.

Flowers said Ciarfardini only winked at her.

She was also given the pen with Ratterman's name on it by someone else to use to corroborate her story. She said she was promised protection to give her false testimony at the trial, as well as rewards, such as a trip to Puerto Rico. There were also "threats," she said from people only identified as "racket boys" in the article.

Ratterman said he was grateful for Flowers coming forward with information "to confirm my innocence."

It was not all good news for Ratterman — the anti-reform candidates (they labeled themselves as the "liberal" candidates), were also drawing large crowds and many predicted that with a split vote among the three sheriff candidates (a Democrat, a Republican and the independent Ratterman), the reform candidate would not garner enough votes to win.

Ratterman went into the lion's den days before the election, making a surprise appearance at a rally of several hundred members of the City Businessmen and Taxpayers League. He was greeted by boos and even a shout of "drop dead," from the crowd. He spoke only briefly before he left with an escort of several police officers.

The "liberal" candidates proceeded to attack the other reform candidates, who did not attend the meeting, as being bad for Newport business and dishonest.

A day later, there was another major announcement that reform was being taken seriously — the federal grand jury indicted six individuals on charges that they violated Ratterman's civil rights: Carinci, new Newport Police Chief Upshere White, the Newport detective Ciarfardini, attorney Lester, the Tropicana's "Marty" Buccieri, and another Newport Police detective, Joseph Quitter.

The grand jury wrote that "The foul odors of vice, corruption, and bribery cover Campbell County officialdom like a pall." It also indicated its probe into Newport corruption would continue.

The banner headlines in Kentucky newspapers concerning the indictments shared space with the news that a Lexington college student, Betty Gail Brown, had been brutally murdered. (See Chapter 9).

The charges against the men were misdemeanors but carried up to a $1,000 fine and a year in jail on each of the two counts they were charged with.

At a large rally days before the election, Ratterman warned to expect a new slander campaign against him and said that his opponents would likely pass down the word on which of his two opponents they should support to avoid a split vote.

On election day, massive crowds turned out in Campbell County — it was anyone's guess which way the voters were leaning.

It turned out voters in Newport decided to support the status quo — the reform candidates for city commission all lost to the "liberal" anti-reform candidates.

But across wider Campbell County, Ratterman cruised to victory for sheriff. The Democratic and Republican candidates each garnered just shy of 7,000 votes each while Ratterman got more than 12,000.

Ratterman wasted no time cracking down, as best he could, on Newport vice. Unlike previous attempts to clean up Newport, however, Ratterman had the strong support of the state and federal governments, as well as newly emboldened local officials. Arrests and indictments soon flowed like watered-down whiskey in Newport's strip clubs.

Seeing the writing on the wall, many of the "racket boys" packed up and left Newport. Many wound up in the country's fastest growing "sin city" — Las Vegas.

In light of the high-profile case, famed New York writer Jimmy Breslin visited Newport and wrote a lengthy piece for *Saga* magazine. He wrote that after the election and crackdowns, Newport was now "locked tighter than a bank." When Breslin went in search of Carinci for an interview, he found a shuttered Tropicana Club instead.

Many of the gambling dens and lounges that didn't shut down converted to relatively tame strip clubs. Some criminal activity of course continued through even the 2000s in Newport. But today the city is better known as a tourist destination than as Kentucky's notorious Sin City.

The cleanup effort was perhaps inevitable – but was no doubt kicked into high gear by the bungled attempt to use an exotic dancer to frame a football star.

Chapter 8

BACK IN LITTLE CHICAGO ....

As the Newport corruption, and the battle against it, progressed, Bowling Green bombings continued on an almost weekly basis.

In August of 1961, a dynamite bomb in a sewer pipe caused widespread damage at Toby's Place tavern downtown — it was the eighth bombing in 11 months. Just days later, five sticks of unexploded dynamite were found under a car. Police Chief Horace Snell announced he was assigning both the department's two detectives, Harry Ashby and Wayne Constant, to probe the bombings, and city officials began discussing increasing the $2,500 reward offered for information about the crimes.

In anticipation of a grand jury investigation into the bombings, Bill Siddens, whose music shop had been bombed months earlier, told reporters that the bombings were started by competing bootleggers and had since expanded as the result of various grudges. He added that he believed there were some 150 bootleggers working in Bowling Green at the height of prohibition, selling 300 cases of whiskey per week. At $1.50 profit per half pint, that meant the bootleggers were pulling in about $20,000 profit per week — equivalent today to about $200,000, or $2.4 million per year.

A community stalwart for decades, 90-year-old Judge John B. Rodes was among those leading the push for an end to the bombings.

The effort seemed to pay off when, in September, three men, Joe David Steenbergen, George Allen and Willis Alford, were indicted by a grand jury. The men allegedly had a hand in several of the local bombings. Alford was a former city police officer. The grand jury also issued an indictment related to slot machines and raised concerns that city police officers were being hired based on political considerations and that there was a lack of leadership in the city police department.

The indictments no doubt gave rise to some hope that the recent crime spree would be blunted by the indictments.

Those hopes were bludgeoned with a shocking discovery just days after the grand jury indictments.

Two farmers were driving across a small bridge over Trammel Creek in a rural area 12 miles south of Bowling Green. As they crossed, they saw a large object floating near the surface of the creek some 50 feet away in an area that was a popular swimming hole. As they got closer, they saw it was a body.

Police arrived and pulled out the corpse, which had been weighted down with a 75-pound grinding stone tied to the body with cotton plow ropes.

The body was covered with bruises and abrasions, and there was a bullet hole in the head. Police immediately had a strong suspicion of who the murder victim was. Billy Graham Jr., charged in the bombing of the Siddens Music Company, had not appeared in court as scheduled the previous week, and police had had no luck tracking him down.

Police asked Graham's ex-wife to identify the body. She quickly confirmed it was her ex-husband.

Coroner Cliff Raymer determined the body had been in the water for several days. Graham had been shot in the right temple, and had suffered a terrific beating, perhaps with a hammer or similar object, before he was executed. Bloody drag marks on the bridge indicated Graham had been beaten and killed somewhere else and then dragged from a car and dumped in the creek.

The obvious motive for the murder was assumed to be Graham's involvement in the bombings. One police officer ominously told reporters the murder was likely "just the beginning" of a battle between those behind the bombings and the community.

A *Daily News* columnist noted that there was an underlying fear for the future of the city, and the reach of criminals was seen in the difficulty in seating local juries in criminal cases in recent months. While many potential jurors claimed to have obligations that prevented them from serving, the unspoken reality was that many people were afraid to pass judgment on the increasingly violent criminals. Graham's brutal murder was a stark warning that the criminals would stop at nothing to protect their enterprises.

Not surprisingly, as the investigation progressed, police reported they were having little luck identifying any suspects. The motive for the murder soon became pretty clear — Graham, police learned, had been telling friends that he knew there was a $2,500 bounty for his death because of what he knew about the bombings.

In October, two men, Selva Wright, 52, and his 28-year-old son Bobby, were arrested on conspiracy charges related to the Siddens bombing. The men admitted they had some sort of business relationship with Graham, and Selva had a previous conviction for moonshining, but they denied the allegations that they were involved in the recent bombings in an interview with reporters.

But the Wrights' connection to Graham became clearer at a preliminary hearing later that month. An 11-year-old son of a tenant farmer testified in front of a packed courtroom that he could identify the grindstone that had been tied to Graham's body. It had a peculiar set of grooves from where the boy had used a metal plow point to stop it from rotating, he said. The stone had been on the farm where the boy and his family had lived the previous year. The farm was now occupied by the Wrights.

The boy's father backed up the testimony, and members of Billy Graham's family testified that the dead man and the Wrights were acquainted. In fact, when the men were arrested, Bobby Wright admitted they had paid a Bowling Green lawyer $350 to represent Graham on the bombing charges.

A friend of Graham's testified that after his arrest, Graham had become an informant for police.

There was also testimony that the elder Wright, Graham and another man had been drinking at the A&W Cafe when Graham started talking about the bombings. Wright told Graham to "shut his mouth or he would get in trouble."

Attorney Paul Huddleston was allowed to address the court, despite his only involvement in the case being in representing the Graham family. He pleaded for a high bond for the Wrights, noting that Graham was out on a $1,000 bond when he was killed. He said it was clear that others were involved in the murder, and the Wrights were a key to determining who they were.

"The individuals involved have shown they will stop at nothing, not even murder," Huddleston said.

The attorney representing the Wrights pointed out that the men were not being charged with murder and objected to the wide range of testimony related not to the bombing, but Graham's death.

The judge agreed with Huddleston, setting bond at an unusually high $25,000.

One person who was on the witness list for the hearing failed to appear. Everett Hardcastle had apparently skipped town, police said. He was found and arrested ten days later. He admitted that he had been in Indiana at the time of the hearing as he feared for his safety. When police searched his 1954 convertible, they found bloodstains in the back seat. They took samples and sent them off to the FBI lab to see if they matched Graham's blood type.

As police awaited the results, 1962 came in with a familiar event. Judge Rodes urged a newly empaneled grand jury to probe the bombings and two killings, that of Graham and a previously unreported murder where a man named Pat Sullivan was found beaten to death in his home in December.

In January, the grand jury issued a report — urging the next grand jury to continue the probe into the bombings and murders.

The veil of fear and secrecy shrouding the criminal activity would clearly be hard to lift.

As Bowling Green struggled with violence, 160 miles away, a brutal murder in Lexington also made national headlines.

Chapter 9

WHO KILLED THE CO-ED?

While there were many contenders for the most notorious crime of the 1960s in southcentral Kentucky, there was a high-profile case in Lexington that continues to be discussed today.

Transylvania University, commonly referred to as Transy, sits in the shadow of the University of Kentucky in Lexington. While much lesser known than the state's flagship school, Transylvania produced two future vice presidents and was known then, as now, for its academics.

Its quaint campus in 1961 was home to a few hundred students. One was Betty Gail Brown, an attractive and popular 19-year-old sophomore who was a French major. Betty sang in the school choir and taught Sunday school at a local church.

October 16, 1961, passed normally for Betty with classes before she returned to her parent's nearby home, where she lived while attending school.

That night, she drove back to campus to study for a biology test with some friends. The study session went late, and she was seen leaving campus just after midnight, when an acquaintance stopped briefly to talk to her as she sat in her car.

She never made it home.

Her concerned mother decided to look for her on campus, so she made the short drive there around 12:40 a.m. After driving through the campus several times, she returned home about an hour later hoping to see her daughter's car.

When it wasn't there, her parents began making frantic calls to see if they could track her down. When that failed, they called the police to report her missing.

Around 3 a.m., a police detective responding to the call made a grisly discovery. He saw a car matching the description of Betty's parked near a campus building.

As he approached, he made out a figure in the driver's seat. As he got closer, he saw it was a young woman, apparently dead, with her head slumped unnaturally over the back of the seat. What turned out to be her bra was wrapped around her neck.

The body was quickly confirmed to be that of Betty Gail Brown. Examination showed she had some abrasions on her body and a cut on her forehead. There was a bloodstain on the dashboard, and some unidentified fingerprints that could be those of the killer.

An autopsy confirmed Betty had been killed by being strangled by her bra, which was ripped, apparently from the strain of being used to kill her.

Surprisingly, the rest of her clothing seemed untouched, and there were no signs of a sexual assault or robbery.

News of the murder made statewide headlines.

The *Lexington Leader*'s banner story the next day featured a large photo of Betty, the blood-smeared dashboard and even a photo of her car with her lifeless body, head slumped over the back of the seat.

Articles at the time and in the months ahead invariably noted that Betty was "attractive" or "pretty." The *Lexington Herald* reported that the killing "has attracted more public interest than any since" a 1941 murder of a well-known female pro golfer and her mother. Newspapers across the state published photos of the car and portraits of Betty.

As was common in such high-profile cases, a slew of tips poured quickly into the police department. Police initially zeroed in on a campus maintenance worker as a suspect, but he was quickly cleared. State police joined the investigation, bolstering the 19 Lexington police detectives already working the case.

Police at first announced they would fingerprint all male Transylvania students, which was later changed to a voluntary program.

The effort again proved a dead end.

Police interviewed the young men who had dated Betty, continued to follow up on tips and even took into consideration the rumors that, for some reason, Betty's own mother had killed her. Amid the persistent rumors that they were somehow involved in the death of their daughter, her parents took lie detector tests in November. Police announced the couple passed the tests and reiterated that the parents were not suspects.

But another suspect did emerge at the time.

A "mental patient" in Bowling Green had been arrested on charges of vagrancy. When police first stopped the man, he explained that he had gotten the cash he was carrying from a woman in Lexington. But after further investigation, police determined he was not the killer.

While the search for Betty's killers continued, years passed with no break.

Then, in 1965, a shocking development in the case came from across the country — Klamath Falls, Oregon.

Alex Arnold Jr., 33, was a former Lexington resident who once worked as a horse trainer and groomer. He was also a Korean War veteran.

He had made his way to Oregon that January, where he was arrested one night for being drunk in public. While in jail, Arnold apparently began experiencing delirium tremens — the sudden and usually severe mental and physical reaction to someone ending alcohol consumption after a stint of heavy drinking.

Arnold asked to speak to a detective, saying he wanted to get something off his chest.

The something was a — sort of — murder confession. While there were a few differences in the subsequent accounts he provided of that night, generally they followed the same outline:

"It seems like a dream, but the longer I think about it the more certain I am that I killed her," Arnold reportedly said in reference to Betty Gail Brown.

"I was drunk and trying to get home. I got as far as Transylvania and passed out. When I came to, I was under a bush. There was a slug of wine left in the bottle, and I drank it," he said.

Arnold said he then stood up with an urge to smoke.

"Then I wanted a cigarette but didn't have a match."

Arnold said he noticed a small car parked nearby. When he approached it, he saw two women inside who were "embracing."

He interrupted them by asking if they had a match. One of the women then "cursed" at him, Arnold said.

"That made me mad, so I jerked open the door on the driver's side. One of the women jumped out and ran and the other tried to get away. I pushed her and she struck her head against the dashboard. It knocked her unconscious.

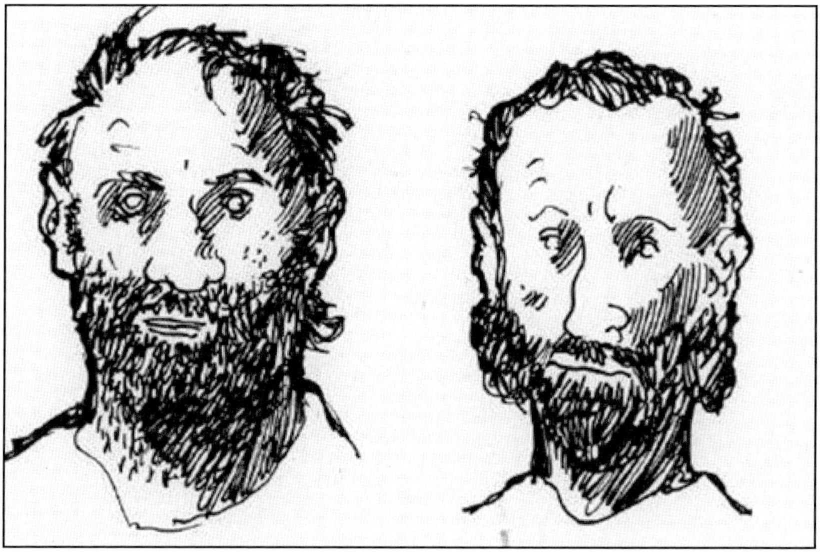

An unknown artist's drawing of the Harpe brothers, Micajah (left) and Wiley.

An undated photo of three Kentucky moonshiners with their still. Credit: WKU Library Special Collections.

An undated photo of legendary federal agent William B. "Big Six" Henderson busting a moonshine operation. Credit: WKU Library Special Collections.

Police investigate at the murder scene with the arrow indicating where Barbara Crouse's body was found. Credit: Bowling Green Daily News.

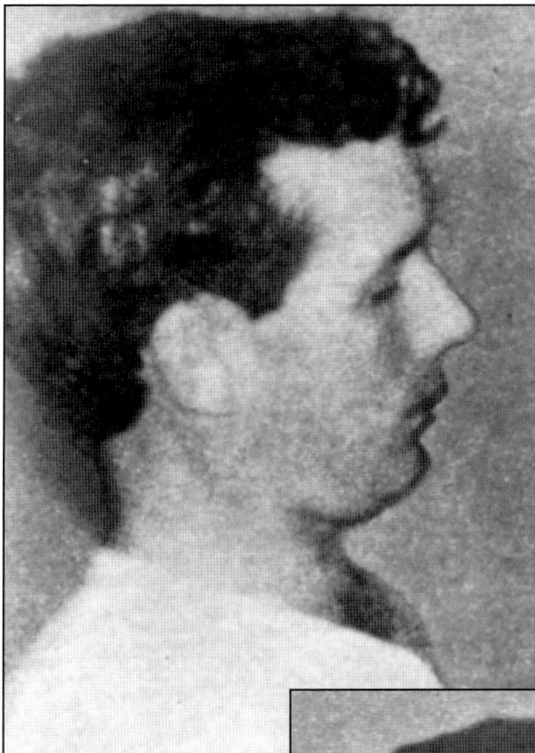

Photos of Robert Crouse (left) and Barbara Crouse (below) released by law enforcement. Credit: Bowling Green Daily News.

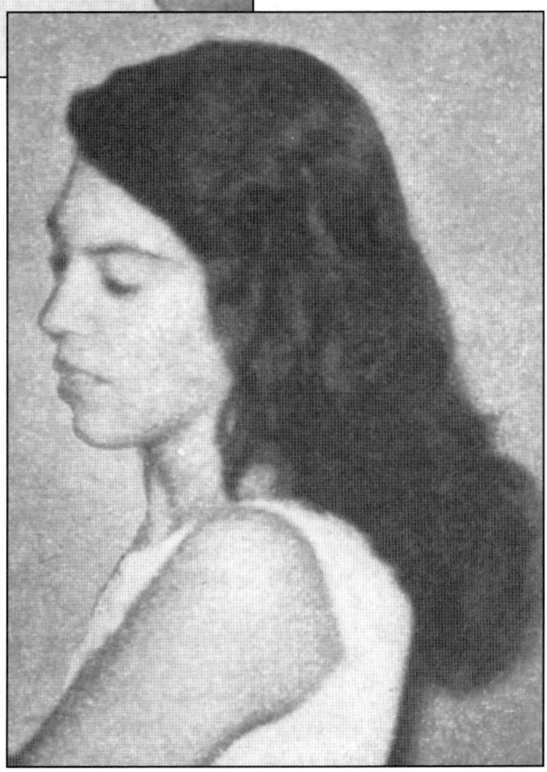

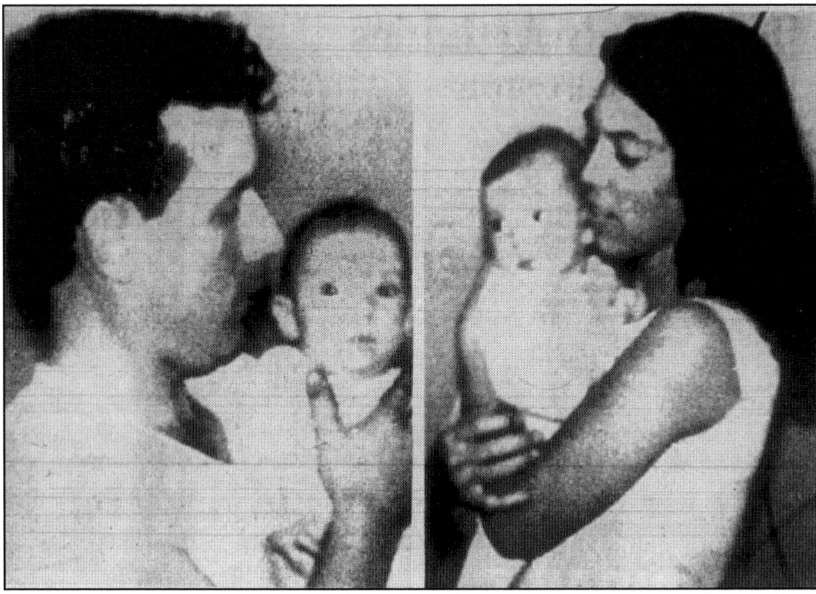

Robert and Barbara Crouse with Dotty in photos released by law enforcement. Credit: Bowling Green Daily News.

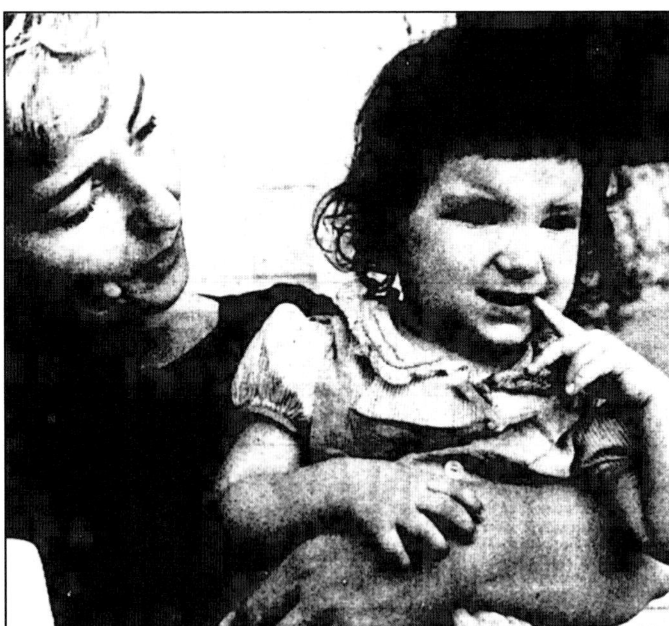

The wife of the Butler County Coroner holds 2-year-old Dotty Crouse the morning her mother was found slain by the side of the road. Credit: Bowling Green Daily News.

Logan County Deputy Sheriff Clyde Darden holds a .32 caliber bullet found next to the body of Barbara Crouse. Credit: Bowling Green Daily News.

A pair of men at the sinkhole where the body of Robert Crouse was found in the Garrett Hollow section of Warren County. Credit: Bowling Green Daily News.

Members of law enforcement examine a body found in a sinkhole in May 1966. The body turned out to be that of Robert Crouse. Credit: Bowling Green Daily News.

Charles Richards is arrested in 1968 and charged with the murder of Robert Crouse. Credit: Bowling Green Daily News.

Edgar Harper

Ella Givens

Searchers at the scene where the bodies of Edgar Harper and Ella Givens were found. Credit: Russellville News-Democrat & Leader.

State Police investigator Guy McMillen.

Vane Brown points to the area where the bodies of Edgar Harper and Ella Givens were found. Credit: Russellville News-Democrat & Leader.

New Logan County Sheriff Jim Johnson (left), who made solving the Harper-Givens murders a priority, is shown with KSP Detective William Smith. Credit: Russellville News-Democrat & Leader.

Edward Harper reads about the discovery of the bodies of his father and sister. Credit: Russellville News-Democrat & Leader.

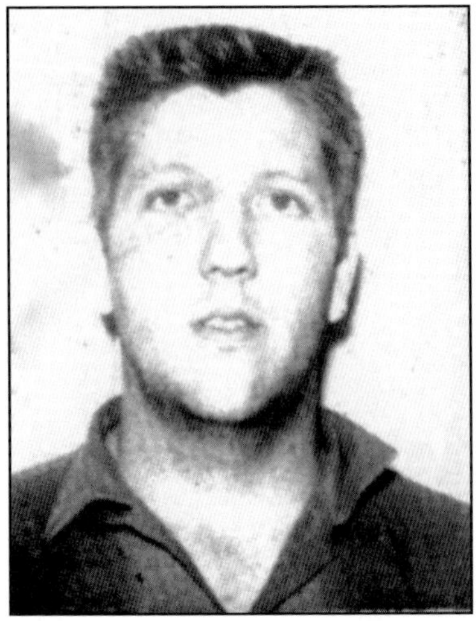

An Alfred Finley Harvey mugshot. Credit: Russellville News-Democrat & Leader.

Logan County Sheriff Gene Sweatt (with a newspaper photographer in the background) near where the bodies of Edgar Harper and Ella Givens were found near the Martin cemetery. Credit: Russellville News-Democrat & Leader.

Sheriff Jim Johnson escorts Kenneth Almon into the Logan County Courthouse after his arrest. Credit: Russellville News-Democrat & Leader.

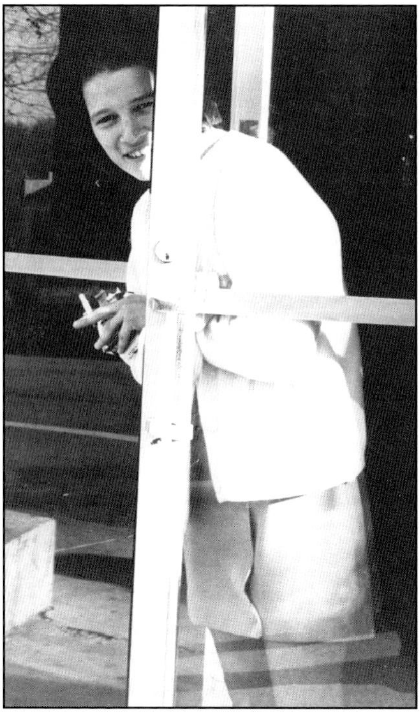

Above: Key witness Carolyn Brown takes a smoke break during the trial at the Christian County Courthouse. Credit: Russellville News-Democrat & Leader.

Top right: Alfred Finley Harvey, with cigar in handcuffed hand, on his way to the Christian County Courthouse for the start of trial. Credit: Russellville News-Democrat & Leader.

Right: Logan Deputy Sheriff Arnold Heltsley escorts James Taylor Lovan for the start of his trial. Credit: Russellville News-Democrat & Leader.

James Taylor Lovan smiles after his not guilty verdict. Credit: Russellville News-Democrat & Leader.

Judge Fuqua accepts the guilty plea of Alfred Finley Harvey as Sheriff Jim Johnson looks on. Credit: Russellville News-Democrat & Leader.

A barbed-wire fence still surrounds the Martin cemetery separating it and the area where the bodies were discovered. Credit: Wes Swietek.

The Martin cemetery as it appears in 2025. Credit: Wes Swietek.

The approximate area at the Martin cemetery where Edgar Harper and Ella Givens were killed, pictured in 2025. Credit: Wes Swietek.

The now shuttered Lewisburg Bank building. Credit: Wes Swietek.

Finney Richards in Bowling Green police headquarters in 1967 as they investigate one of the dozens of shootings Richards was involved in. Credit: Bowling Green Daily News.

Finney Richards shows a head laceration at BG police headquarters to police after another shooting. He was subsequently charged with murder. Credit: Bowling Green Daily News.

Barbara Flatt (Purkerson) in her engagement photo in 1956. Credit: Bowling Green Daily News.

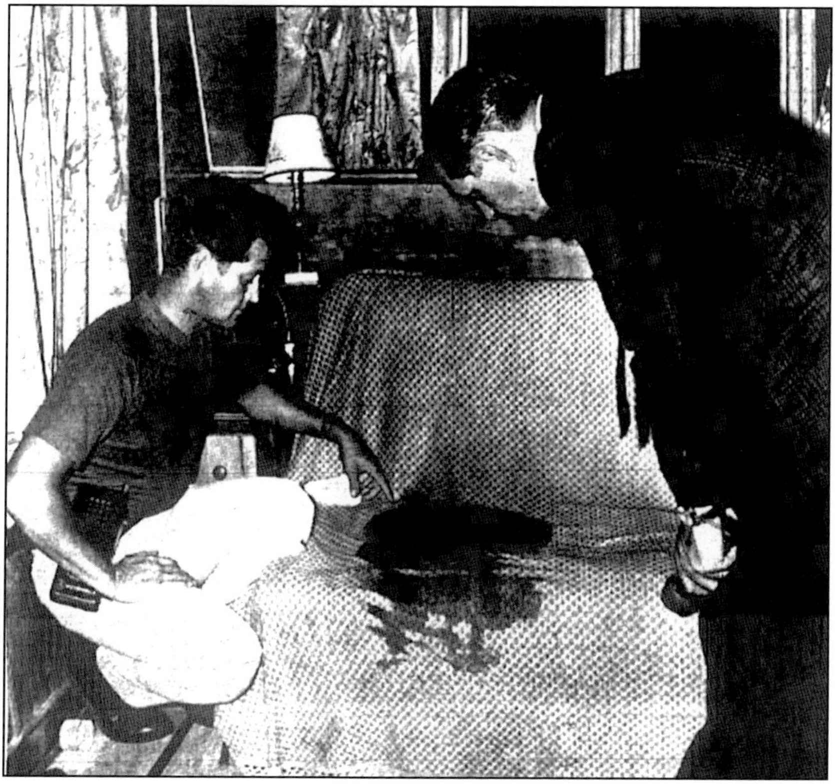

Investigators examine the blood-stained couch where Finney Richards was shot. Credit: Bowling Green Daily News.

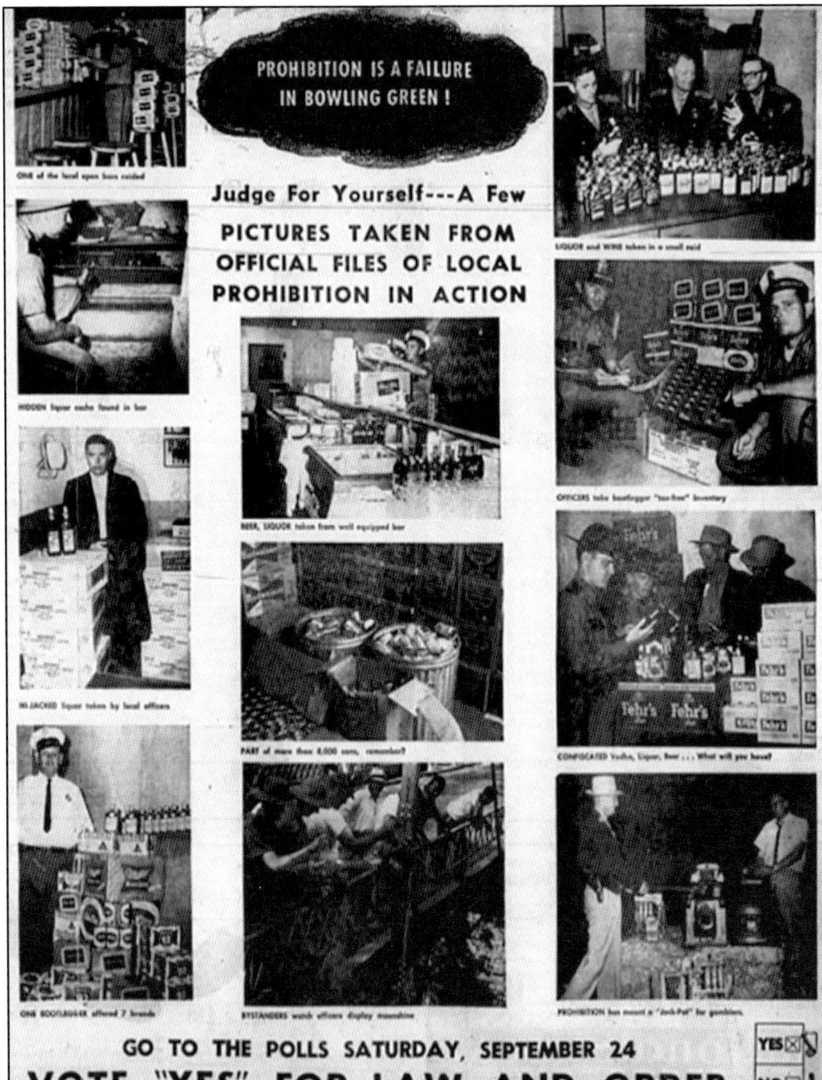

A newspaper ad in 1960 calling for a yes vote to return legal alcohol sales to Bowling Green. Credit: Bowling Green Daily News.

Billie (sometimes spelled Billy) Graham in a police photo.

The body of Billy Graham is pulled out of Trammell Creek. His body was weighed down with a large grindstone. Credit: Bowling Green Daily News.

Beer and whiskey seized by Bowling Green police after a 1960 raid at a city residence. Credit: Bowling Green Daily News.

Joe Steenbergen (center) after his arrest on charges of blowing up a Bowling Green bar in 1961. Credit: Bowling Green Daily News.

Police in 1963 examine a bomb left under the car of Bowling Green Police Department detective Wayne Constant, who was named the city's new police chief the previous day. *Credit:* Bowling Green Daily News.

Another frequent sight in Bowling Green was stolen cars, some with parts stripped. *Credit:* Bowling Green Daily News.

After another murder victim was pulled from the waters of Barren River, this sign was placed by an unknown individual near the Old Richardsville Road bridge. Credit: Bowling Green Daily News.

George Ratterman with his wife and eight children in 1961. Credit: Cincinnati Enquirer.

George Ratterman displays his torn pants to reporters as he discusses his arrest the previous night. Credit: Cincinnati Enquirer.

George Ratterman and his wife Anne, along with friend Thomas Paisley, after George Ratterman's arrest. Credit: Cincinnati Enquirer.

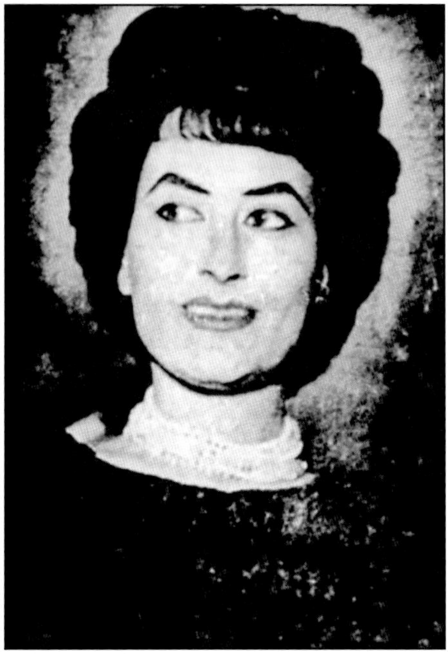

Exotic dancer April Flowers. Credit: Cincinnati Enquirer.

April Flowers in her "slave girl" costume. Credit: Cincinnati Enquirer.

Exotic dancer Rita Desmond. Credit: Cincinnati Enquirer.

In court, from left, are Anne and George Ratterman, April Flowers, Tito Carinci and Rita Desmond. Credit: Cincinnati Enquirer.

George Ratterman gets a kiss from wife Anne after winning his case. Credit: Cincinnati Enquirer.

The testimony of photographer Tom Withrow (right) was the key to the case. Credit: Cincinnati Enquirer.

Tito Carinci. Credit: Cincinnati Enquirer.

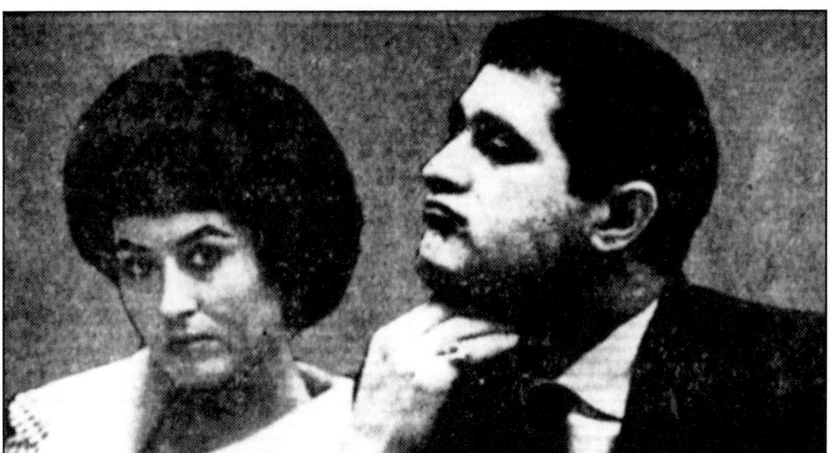

April Flowers and Tito Carinci in court. The pair were at the center of numerous investigations regarding Newport corruption. Credit: Cincinnati Enquirer.

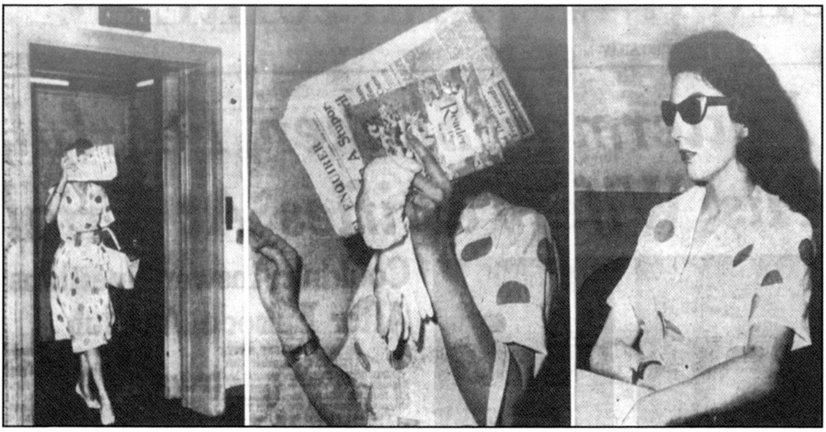

Rita Desmond hides from a photographer after a court proceeding. Credit: Cincinnati Enquirer.

Marion Parker Duke, center, shares a laugh in April, 1953, as he prepares for his murder trial. With Duke on the steps of the Warren County Jail are, from left, defense attorney Leland H. Logan, Jailer Raymond McClard, Duke's defense attorney Rodes K. Myers, and Deputy Jailer Oscar "Doc" Isbell. Credit: Bowling Green Daily News.

The shattered remains of the Moody house on Henry Avenue in Bowling Green after it was destroyed by a dynamite blast on Feb. 16, 1972. Credit: Courtesy of the Moody family.

Bowling Green Police Detective Capt. Darrell Moody and his wife Betty outside their home on Henry Avenue that was destroyed by a dynamite blast on Feb. 16, 1972.

In an undated photo, Kentucky State Police Trooper William Barrett stands outside the home where he was killed Dec. 19, 1971. Credit: Bowling Green Daily News.

Cracked blacktop is all the remains of the notorious Burke's Alley in Bowling Green. Credit: Wes Swietek.

"Then I got scared," Arnold said. "I climbed in the back seat and got the bra and put it around her neck and strangled her. Then I kissed her breast and then buttoned up the blouse so no one would think it was a sex killing. Then I buttoned her blouse and ran."

Arnold said he then went to an acquaintance's house for the night. He subsequently wandered across the country before winding up in Oregon.

Upon being informed of the confession, Lexington police started looking into his story. They confirmed that Arnold had lived a little more than a mile from the Transy campus at the time of the murder. He also had a criminal record.

While some police officials publicly cast doubt on Arnold's story, they decided to send detectives to Oregon to interview him in person.

When they first spoke to him, Arnold again said he was "99 percent" sure he had killed the coed. The detectives spent two days quizzing Arnold before being satisfied that he had indeed killed Betty Gail Brown.

He eventually hand wrote and signed a confession that elaborated on what he said happened that night.

After getting drunk, Arnold said he had wandered on to the Transylvania campus and took a nap. After waking up, he began walking across campus and saw a car. Inside, "I seen what looked like two woman (sic) making love. They were hugging and kissing each other," he wrote, then again related how he asked for a match to light a cigarette.

"They began to cuss me. I said pardon me and started on for Short and Broadway. As I walked on, they continued to cuss me. Being drunk and on the spur of the moment, I got mad and turned back to the car. Jerking the door open on the driver's side I grabbed the girl on the driver's side as she was leaning away from me. The other girl opened the door and run," he wrote.

Arnold then elaborated in grisly detail what he did to Betty.

"Hitting the girl's head against the dashboard I either knocked her out or she fainted. Jerking her head back against the seat by her hair and shoulders I realized she was out. Getting scared and being drunk I opened the back door and got in the back seat. Picking up her brassier that was laying over the back of the seat I hung it around her neck and strangled her by putting my hands on each end of the brassier and putting my knee against the back of the seat for leverage. I held it there for about a minute and a half. The only thing that she did was quiver a little bit.

"I throwed (sic) the brassier in the front seat and closed the front door. I noticed that the blouse was open all the way down. I climbed in the front seat to button it up because I thought if she was found that way they would think I tried to rape her thinking sure I would be caught. As I was buttoning up the blouse from the bottom up and being crazy drunk I thought what a cute little son of a bitch you are and kissed her lightly on the top of the breast."

Arnold then said he left the vehicle and went to the home of a female acquaintance, Mae Hedges. He said he told her he had killed a woman, but Hedges didn't believe him. He then passed out.

The Lexington detectives felt Arnold's confession contained information only the killer would know and quickly obtained an arrest warrant. Arnold said he would not fight extradition back to the Bluegrass state, although he eventually pleaded not guilty.

Almost four years exactly after Betty Gail Brown's murder, the trial of Alex Arnold began in a packed courtroom in Lexington.

The prosecution could easily prove that Betty was murdered, but the seemingly only evidence that Arnold was the perpetrator was the confession. So, when the prosecution moved to admit the confession into the trial, Arnold's defense lawyers objected, arguing that Arnold's mental condition at the time of the confession prevented him from understanding his rights.

The presiding judge decided to hear from Arnold himself (outside of the presence of the jury) before ruling on the matter.

Arnold said he had many confused thoughts and dreams at the time of the confession — including that there was a "mind-reading machine" outside his cell, but said he gave the confession voluntarily.

After also hearing from the detectives and a doctor who had interacted with Arnold, the judge ruled the confession was admissible.

The seemingly damning confession was then read to the jury by police detectives during their testimony. The defense tried to cast doubt on Arnold's memory by getting detectives to admit that some details he had talked about with them were seemingly inaccurate — such as that there was a red thermos in the back seat of Betty's car, and that he closed all the car doors by pushing buttons that Betty's car was not equipped with. Arnold also at some point said he threw the bra in the backseat when it had been found around her neck.

Also, the defense pointed out that none of the fingerprints found in the car matched Arnold's.

But because Arnold's own words were seemingly strong evidence against him, the defense took the risky step of calling him to testify.

Wearing a new suit his mother had purchased for him, Arnold relayed to jurors a troubled childhood and drinking problem after returning from Korea, which had led to several arrests.

His defense attorney then came to the primary question — the circumstances surrounding his confession.

Arnold said he had spent so much time drinking that he was essentially delusional, citing his belief that a machine was reading his mind while locked up. As for how he seemingly knew so much about the crime, he said while he had been locked up in Lexington, on unrelated charges of steering clients to prostitutes, he shared a cell with a man who had been an initial suspect in the Brown killing. Arnold said the man had given him some information on the case.

The story was of course extensively covered in newspapers and Arnold said he and Green discussed the case repeatedly.

Arnold then said while he once did believe he may have killed Betty, he now believed differently. He cited the small discrepancies, such as the buttons in the car and where the bra was found, as why he now believed his confession was — probably — a delusion.

Asked point-blank whether he killed Betty Gail Brown, Arnold said he couldn't rule out that he had, but he didn't "think I did."

The prosecution, however, under cross examination got Arnold to admit he had confessed voluntarily and had him repeat the lurid details he had originally given as to what transpired that night.

Describing how Betty quivered while he strangled her was undoubtedly a strong point for the prosecution case.

After Arnold, the defense called Mae Hedges to the stand. Hedges said Arnold had not come to her house on the night of the murder and had never said anything about killing a woman.

Arnold's aunt then testified, saying Arnold had in fact stayed in her home the night of the murders. The prosecution pointed out that the aunt had only come forward with this supposed alibi in recent weeks, even though she knew for months her nephew was on trial for murder.

A man who claimed he had been in the area the night of the murder and saw a suspicious-looking man near the scene also testified that the man he saw was not Arnold.

Finally, the defense sought to further discredit the confession by casting doubt on the claim that Betty was being intimate with another woman.

Various witnesses testified to Betty's "good character," and reported how she had casually dated various boys.

Her parents also testified, saying she had never given any indication of being attracted to women.

After closing arguments, the jury began deliberations. After a few hours, the jury reported it was deadlocked — reportedly five guilty votes and seven not guilty. The judge declared a mistrial and the case was slated to be retried, but never was. Prosecutors undoubtedly questioned pursuing a case where most jurors were for acquittal.

Arnold died in 1980, with the question of his guilt or innocence never settled.

In the years since Arnold's trial, various theories and suspects have emerged in the case, including in 2010, when a serial killer named Nolan Ray George was identified as a person of interest in Betty's murder.

George was charged with killing several women, usually by strangling them with articles of their own clothing. His first known victim was found in 1969 strangled in a car, like Betty Gail Brown.

It wasn't until around 2010 that he was linked to several other murders of women by strangulation.

Aside from the same method of killing, George became a logical suspect in the Lexington case because he was from London, Kentucky, only about 80 miles from Lexington. He would have been around 18 at the time of Betty's killing.

But like other leads and theories (and even one detailed confession), the George speculation never led to charges, and the question of who killed Betty Gail Brown remains one of the Bluegrass state's enduring mysteries.

Chapter 10

BOWLING GREEN AS A "BOOM TOWN"

In Bowling Green, there was hope that some information about the bombings would finally be revealed when the Wrights went to trial in April of 1961. But rather than a probe that could reveal details about the crime spree, it was a formality as the Wrights pleaded guilty to bombing the Siddens Music Company. They were ordered to serve three months in jail and fined $500 each.

As part of the agreement, the Wrights agreed to take lie-detector tests regarding the bombings. Police were still hoping that the Wrights could help them figure out who was behind the bombings and Graham's murder, but the tests apparently failed to shed any light on those crimes.

Siddens, meanwhile, had apparently left town for a safer location.

That June, a Bowling Green police captain, William Brumit, went public with an allegation that police chief Horace Snell had ordered police to stop inspecting beer halls for criminal activity. When Brumit protested, he said, Snell removed him as a shift leader.

Days later, in front of an overflow crowd of more than 350 concerned citizens in a local courtroom, city officials held a public hearing on the allegations.

Snell, who was represented by an attorney, did not testify. Brumit said Snell claimed police had more pressing issues than illegal beer sales, such as the notorious brothel being openly run by Pauline Tabor on Clay Street near downtown. Snell also said, according to Brumit, that a continued crackdown on the beer joints "might start the bombing again."

The city commission ultimately ordered Snell to restore Brumit to his role as shift commander and to resume inspecting beer halls. The order drew applause from the large crowd.

A week later, someone threw a Molotov cocktail at the police department headquarters in the middle of the night. The flame quickly went out and the device did little damage.

In December, record lows dropped to 8-below zero in Bowling Green, and snow and freezing temperatures covered much of the country. Like the temperatures, the violence took a deep dive in the latter half of 1962, the spree of bombings and still unsolved murder of Graham no longer making headlines.

As 1963 dawned, the headlines were instead focused on a lawsuit filed by 19 Warren County families seeking the desegregation of local schools. In an effort to put off a desegregation effort such as that seen across the South, the city school system had just spent $75,000 renovating the all-Black High Street High School.

The unusually cold winter continued with a new record of 21-below zero in late January. A sheet of ice covered the usually fast-flowing Barren River. In April, a federal judge ordered Bowling Green schools be desegregated, and chastised local officials for fighting the integration of local schools. Warren County schools soon followed with integration; unlike the school desegregation efforts making national headlines in 1963, the local integration of schools was largely peaceful. And despite wide national unrest over civil rights, the summer of 1963 was also largely peaceful in southcentral Kentucky.

That changed in late August.

One of the leaders of the city police investigation into the bombings was a police detective named Wayne Constant. Constant, a former Warren County Sheriff's deputy, had been with Bowling Green police for six years. An Edmonson County native, the 39-year-old Constant was known as a by-the-books officer with a gruff exterior but a generous nature.

Earlier in 1963, the controversial Snell had retired as police chief, and Constant was one of the men who applied to fill the top spot. At an often-heated public meeting in August, city commissioners met to pick a new chief. At the meeting, a representative of the local Fraternal Order of Police asked that city commissioners avoid political considerations when picking a new chief. The FOP representative said the city police department had been mired in a "political cesspool" in recent years.

The city commission ultimately voted, behind closed doors, 7-5 to appoint Constant as police chief. The chief-to-be worked his usual evening shift and went home around 1:30 a.m., undoubtedly curious as to what awaited him. He got a glimpse a few hours later.

At around 8:30 a.m., he was taking his young daughter to school. As they walked to his car parked in front of his home at 11th and Center Streets, Constant saw an all-too familiar device under his car: six sticks of dynamite taped together and wrapped in cloth. It had rained heavily the previous night, and police surmised the rain had extinguished the long fuse before it reached the bomb's detonator.

The bomb was sent off to the FBI lab for examination.

In an editorial, the *Daily News* speculated that the bomb was intended to send a message that Constant should not be too gung-ho in cracking down on criminal enterprises in the city. As the occasional police busts would reveal, the sale of bootleg alcohol was still a massive business in the region, even though alcohol sales were legal. Police were also regularly confiscating illegal gambling machines from the city's thriving bars and private clubs.

Judge Rodes, now 93, charged a new grand jury the following month to probe the attempted bombing of Constant, as well as the other recent crimes.

"Outlawry, that's what it is, outlawry," Rodes said.

The city commission, meanwhile, formally approved Constant's appointment as chief, this time by an 8-4 vote, His salary was $5,040 a year. The commission also approved offering a $10,000 reward for information about the attempted bombing.

National news at the time became increasingly focused on the fight for civil rights, with school desegregation efforts the (often literal) battleground. The U.S. role in the Vietnam War was also growing, although it was not yet the controversial entanglement it would become.

Then, on November 22, 1963, unthinkable news dwarfed all else: President John F. Kennedy, just 46, was assassinated in Dallas. The *Daily News*, under a massive banner headline "PRESIDENT IS SLAIN," ran a picture of Kennedy's 1960 campaign trip to Bowling Green.

The years ahead, both nationally and in southcentral Kentucky, would be increasingly marked by turbulence, unrest, and crime.

Chapter 11

VIOLENCE TAKES HOLD

In January of 1964, a Warren County grand jury delivered more words about the crime spree of recent years, but only indictments on minor charges. The jury wrote that there was a general public "laxity" about fighting crime in the city. It also said the sheriff's office was understaffed.

The sheriff's office was tasked with covering all areas in the county outside Bowling Green's city limits, encompassing a population of about 15,000, with just five employees, three of whom were deputies.

Sheriff Hubert Phelps said his deputies at times worked 16-hour shifts. The meager law enforcement presence undoubtedly was seen by criminals as an enticement to set up shop in the county. In claiming that its hands were tied in terms of adding more deputies, Warren County's fiscal court cited an archaic state law that stipulated that an outgoing sheriff determined the size of the department.

In August, Bowling Green police detective Capt. Harry Ashby — the other primary investigator with Constant into the bombings in the city — was sitting at his 18th Street home with his wife watching TV at around 9:45 p.m. They heard a muffled sound from outside, but when Ashby went to the window, he saw nothing unusual on the dark street.

The next morning, a neighbor of the Ashbys was walking his dog when he noticed an oil can and some weird debris under his neighbor's car. Closer inspection showed it was a makeshift bomb. A group of Army demolition experts from nearby Fort Knox examined the bomb and found it was composed of 10 sticks of dynamite in an oil can, with two fuses and blasting caps. One of the caps had exploded, leaving a 16-foot circle of debris on the street, but the dynamite had for some unknown reason not detonated.

Despite the seemingly obvious link to the city's other bombings, police publicly speculated that the bomb was perhaps meant to be a diversion. That same night, burglars entered a downtown jewelry store and made away with $1,000 worth of watches and rings.

Just days later, the bombing of liquor-related businesses in Bowling Green resumed. Two sticks of dynamite caused extensive damage after they were thrown on the roof of Cook's Liquor Store at 2:30 a.m., apparently from a passing car. Ashby again downplayed a possible link to the business bombings and the explosives found under his car.

In January, there was another dynamite blast at a tobacco warehouse that was heard throughout the city. Later that month, a grand jury, again tasked with investigating the bombings, failed to issue any indictments. The jury did note that it heard from witnesses who claimed local law enforcement was being paid off by criminals, but the claims could not be proven.

The thought that the new bombings were isolated incidents faded early on the morning of February 11, when a dynamite blast and resulting fire destroyed the buildings used by the McLellan Stone Company just north of the city limits. The explosion around 2:30 a.m. sent debris flying several hundred yards, blocking adjoining roads. The blast was caused by a bomb of 12-15 sticks of dynamite. The business was either set on fire at the same time or the blast ignited parts of the building, which was fully destroyed. Another bomb, made of 12 sticks of dynamite, was found undetonated at the site.

A *Daily News* photo from later that morning shows Ashby, wearing a coat and fedora, casually dismantling the bomb on a makeshift table.

Police said there were some differences in the way the dynamite bombs from the recent incidents were assembled, but Sheriff Phelps said they were likely related — exactly how remained anyone's guess.

A month later, several dynamite blasts destroyed tens of thousands of dollars of construction equipment at a quarry in Simpson County near the Warren County line.

Violence, including many bombings, also dominated national news at the time. The KKK and its supporters were unleashing a wave of violence not seen since Reconstruction against civil rights activists. In many cases, dynamite bombs like those that had hit Bowling Green, were used. Meanwhile, more and more American soldiers were being killed in the jungles of Viet Nam, leading to small protests that would soon swell.

That summer, another member of law enforcement was targeted by a would-be bomber. City policeman Jim Duncan owned a small houseboat named "Miss Carol" that he kept docked off Boatlanding Road on Barren River. Some children playing by the river saw a bomb, made of five sticks of dynamite with a 100-foot fuse, on the boat's deck on a June morning. The bomb had for some reason not detonated, sparing Miss Carol from a watery death. Another city police officer "disposed" of the bomb by simply dropping it into the river.

Bombers returned to the pattern of targeting construction-related businesses a month later, as a massive dynamite bomb destroyed much of the R.E. Gaddie blacktop plant in Bowling Green. The blast was heard throughout much of the city. As had become the norm, police said they did not have suspects or a possible motive.

The stone, blacktop, and related companies in Bowling Green had been especially busy in recent years as new sewer, road, and general construction projects were on the rise. The biggest project, however, was one that would transform the city forever, for good and bad.

In December of 1965, a project years in the making culminated with the official opening of the $10.2 million I-65 corridor from Bowling Green 20 miles south to near the Tennessee border. When the road was continued to Nashville, I-65 became one of the busiest roads in the entire region, bringing thousands of travelers daily through Bowling Green. The corridor brought Bowling Green tremendous prosperity in the years ahead. A side impact, however, was that the road soon became a major transportation route for drugs, stolen vehicles and criminals, many who made stops in the conveniently located growing city that offered a wide variety of vices and opportunities.

That summer of 1965, the FBI announced it would be probing not only the recent Bowling Green bombings, but a pair of dynamite bombs that had targeted the South Central Rural Telephone Cooperative in nearby Glasgow. The latter bombings had a more obvious motivation — workers at the company were in the midst of a strike when the bombings took place.

Meanwhile, Bowling Green's business leaders, undoubtedly chagrined over the lack of prosecutions in the city's bombings that had now spanned several years, offered a $1,000 reward for information in the cases. Citizens National Bank President Top Orendorf, a prominent figure in Bowling Green for decades, announced the reward and urged other business leaders to pitch in to grow the reward fund.

A day later, Orendorf announced that additional businesses were stepping up to meet his challenge. Orendorf said the fund was meant to end "an era of fear" in the community caused by the bombings.

Coincidentally, Sheriff Hubert Phelps announced that same day that deputies had found 40 sticks of dynamite and dozens of blasting caps hidden in an abandoned house on the outskirts of the city.

Within days, the fund stood at more than $9,000 (equivalent to almost $100,000 in 2025) and a public meeting was scheduled to address the issue. On the day of the meeting, about two dozen officials and business leaders showed up — but only three members of the general public. A similar meeting was held the following week, and only 13 people attended. The meager turnouts seemed to underscore the claim that public apathy (or fear) was somewhat to blame for the lack of progress.

"Too many people don't want to get involved," said circuit court judge Robert Coleman.

Both Police Chief Constant and Sheriff Phelps said they lacked adequate resources to fight the crime wave. Constant noted the department had only eight squad cars and two detectives, with a total employee count of about 40, for the city of 32,000; while Phelps reminded the public he had only three road deputies to patrol the remainder of the entire county.

A few days later, a new grand jury was empaneled, and Judge Coleman gave them a familiar task: probe the bombings. A month later, the grand jury released its report and again passed the proverbial buck. No bombing-related indictments were issued; the jurors reported that there simply was not enough evidence for indictments.

Instead, the jurors recommended a special detective or detectives be hired to probe the bombings and chastised those involved: "Our contempt for those who perpetrate such acts is exceeded only by our abhorrence of their crimes, which rape the image of a community."

Coincidentally, the same day that the grand jury issued its report, more than 100 pinball machines were seized from area businesses. It was part of a statewide crackdown on the machines, which were typically used to facilitate gambling. The effort locally was being driven by attorney Paul Huddleston, who had recently been appointed as a special counsel to the state attorney general to lead the fight against pinball machines. Gov. Edward Breathitt said the machines were a primary money maker for organized crime in the state and encouraged juvenile delinquency.

"We want to have them barred as public nuisances," Commonwealth's Attorney Lowe said.

The crackdown led to a bizarre scene: dozens of pinball machines lined neatly up on the sidewalk in front of the Warren County Courthouse. Police, with the aid of some jail inmates, were hauling truckloads of machines to the courthouse, where Huddleston planned to store them.

County Judge-Executive Basil Griffin, however, quickly nixed that plan.

"We are going to take the penny arcade out of the courthouse," he said, and the machines were quickly loaded back onto the trucks

As for the bombings, police thought they had a possible break in late November when some deer hunters stumbled upon a cache of 26 sticks of dynamite and an assembled dynamite bomb near an abandoned quarry near the Simpson-Warren County line.

Sheriff Phelps stationed a deputy in a secluded area nearby in hopes of nabbing the bombers as they came to resupply, but the plans were thwarted when a local radio station reported on the discovery. Some of the materials in the bomb were identical to those used in the recent bombings, as was the maker of the dynamite — the DuPont company.

Phelps claimed the discovery could have cracked the dynamite cases "wide open," but the leak had thwarted that hope.

As 1965 ended, Warren County had a dubious distinction. Despite the slew of high-profile unsolved crimes, Warren County had plenty of arrests on its books. Warren had more residents sentenced to jail time that year than all but two counties — Jefferson, home of Louisville, and Fayette, home of Lexington — but only by a slim margin despite the huge size difference in the counties.

The following year started off quietly, until March of 1966 when a dynamite bomb was found attached to a car in Bowling Green on Nutwood Avenue. The bomb, consisting of two sticks of dynamite, had not detonated.

Bowling Green Police Department detectives Darrell Moody and Fred Lancaster told reporters they planned to administer lie detector tests to two individuals who had emerged as suspects. They also indicated that parts of the unexploded bomb had yielded some physical evidence.

Just days later, another Bowling Green man found a small dynamite detonation device, capable of a small explosion, wired to his car's sparkplugs. Police soon determined the man was looking to annoy his neighbors, with whom he had been squabbling, and decided to fake an attempted bombing of his own.

Along with the sporadic bombings, crime was a regular source for front-page news in 1966 — break-ins, safe cracking, bank robberies, and the like. But there was a sudden surge in stolen car cases; in some cases, vehicle carcasses were found abandoned in rural parts of the county stripped of the most valuable parts; other times the entire vehicle vanished from Warren County forever.

Scorching temperatures that summer caused dozens of deaths across the country; southcentral Kentucky was not immune with numerous days seeing highs reaching 100 or more. The heat seemed to slow down crime — no bombings had been reported in 6 months. That streak ended on a warm August night, when a bomb made of about a dozen sticks of dynamite flattened a wholesale meat distribution company's headquarters just north of the city.

While police issued the usual refrain that there were some potential leads, no arrests would be forthcoming.

A month later, a grand jury reported that it had found "low morale" among local police. The main culprit was low pay. City firefighters that summer had also been pressing for a pay raise, but the city, facing a budget shortfall, was looking at raising taxes just to make ends meet.

The issue came to a head in September when the city commission was debating a tax increase. When a proposed tax hike to fund raises for police and firefighters was voted down, a group of 27 police officers (the entire department had 35) announced they would essentially go on strike at midnight, responding only to emergencies. Fifty of the fire department's 54 members also signed a pledge to go on strike.

A panicked city commission quickly held another vote on a smaller hike, which passed in a first, preliminary reading. Satisfied for the time being that progress was being made, the firefighters and officers called off the work stoppage until the city commission reconvened.

The city eventually proposed a 20 percent pay hike, but police and fire personnel spokesmen said that wasn't enough to avert a work stoppage.

With that issue looming, another bomber struck in Bowling Green. This time several sticks of dynamite exploded at the front door of the Orange Bar. Police speculated that this bombing was related to a personal dispute between the bar owner and an employee.

In early October, city commission members approved a tax hike and a 20 percent increase in pay for emergency workers. Despite previously saying the 20 percent increase was inadequate, police and fire leaders said they would stay on the job.

Police and firefighters soon earned their higher pay.

Someone had taken to abandoning stolen cars on rural Glen Lily Road, stripping them of their Vehicle Identification Number plates and setting them on fire. The cars were presumed to have been stolen from out of state, and it seems likely that the thieves were simply after the VIN plates to put on other stolen vehicles. That the cars — five found in one week — were being abandoned in Bowling Green was the first evidence that a large and well-organized car theft ring was operating in the city.

The same day that a 1964 Ford was found burning on Glen Lily Road in late October, police responded to what was at first thought to be separate, fatal hit and run accidents. A closer look revealed what appeared to be two murders.

In both cases, motorists ran into bodies on rural roads at night; one thought he had struck a dog only to find the body of Elmer Vernice Stinson, 36, of Allen County, in the road. Two men up early on their way to go fishing found the bloody body of Eulyse Julion Carter, 36, of Scottsville, on the side of another rural road.

Police believed that both men had been beaten and killed somewhere else, and their bodies dumped on the roads. Robbery was a possible motive as both men's wallets were missing. Adding to the mystery was the fact that the men were acquainted. The men had been seen at Bowling Green nightspots before their deaths, but not together.

A Bowling Green man later admitted to robbing Stinson, but said he left him by the road, where he was apparently later hit by a car. Police never publicly explained why the original finding that Stinson was killed before his body was hit had changed; Carter's death was also later ruled to be an accident.

The remarkable coincidence that two men, who knew each other, would both die on the same night after being struck by cars on rural roads, was apparently never explored further.

The first months of 1967 saw a bust of a massive cock-fighting operation, complete with bleachers for spectators, numerous burglaries and assaults, and a high-profile case of a Bowling Green woman who shot and killed her husband because, she said, he had been abusive to her and their children.

The incidents and the totality of 1966 crimes led the *Daily News* to ask if the crime rate had gone up in a series of front-page articles. The answer? It depended on who you asked.

"Let's face it, the number of homicides in the city and county is up over last year," police chief Constant said of 1966 compared to the previous year.

But most of those interviewed said the increase in crime was on par with a national spike and mostly the result of a growing city. County Attorney Henry Potter added that many of the violators were "victims of society but some of them are just downright mean."

The tally of recent unsolved murders in Warren County at that point stood at seven and would continue to grow for years.

The spike in violent deaths was dramatic in the early months of 1967:

In January, there was the case of the Bowling Green woman who shot her allegedly abusive husband.

Then in March, Alvaton's only police officer was fatally shot after trying to arrest a man; days later a prominent Horse Cave auto dealer was charged with fatally shooting a restaurant owner in a tiff over a woman.

Within a few days, a Warren man shot and killed his young wife, then turned the gun on himself. A suicide note left by the man accused his wife of cheating on him.

Two days later, a man stabbed and killed his housemate after an argument.

In early April, a 24-year-old Bowling Green man was charged with murder after shooting a 16-year-old girl after a night of drinking.

That made seven people killed in the first 90 days of the new year.

Later that summer, a presidential commission predicted crime would continue to increase nationally. The reason? The "deprivations of ghetto life," a growing population of the age demographic that committed the most crime — people in their late teens and early 20s — and the fact that better crime reporting statistics were now available.

Adding to the somber mood was the growing number of U.S. casualties in the Viet Nam War. Death notices for local soldiers became an almost daily occurrence — along with continued news of civil unrest, mostly in large cities, related to the push for civil rights.

After the unprecedented wave of crime to start the year, the summer of 1967 passed relatively quietly in Bowling Green, save for an August murder and a state trooper being non-fatally shot that fall while responding to a call. But on October 22, the bombings returned.

This time the target was the Cardinal Billiards pool room near the city high school. An estimated three to six sticks of dynamite were placed on an air conditioning unit. The blast around 11 p.m. shattered windows in surrounding blocks, including 45 at the high school. The building was heavily damaged but still standing when hundreds of Western students living in nearby housing came to gawk at the scene. The building was empty when the bomb went off and no one was injured, although a nearby resident reported being literally knocked out of his bed by the shockwave of the blast.

The pool room owner cryptically told reporters he was expecting trouble. Earlier that year someone had fired several shots into the building after closing hours. Police Chief Constant also confirmed that the bombing was not a surprise but declined to elaborate. He did say that he believed the bombing was not related to the other recent bombings.

Two months later, the peace of a quiet residential street was shattered as two sticks of dynamite exploded in a home's garage. No one was injured, and police quickly determined that the bomb was intended for someone else as the home was occupied by a doctor and his family with no known enemies.

That January, a grand jury was — once again — tasked with probing the bombings and unsolved murders. Constant said that the more recent bombings were likely a result of personal "grudges," while the older bombings were the work of the city's hardcore criminal element. Both Constant and sheriff Watts took the opportunity to say they were stymied in their investigations by a lack of manpower.

The year ended with more meetings of a local grand jury. Chief Constant confirmed to reporters he spent more than an hour testifying, and numerous other law enforcement officials were expected to do the same. But as had become the norm, when the grand jury handed down more than 30 indictments days later, none were related to the bombings.

There were behind the scenes moves, however, to finally get some indictments related to the more severe violence. An unnamed city official revealed to the Daily News that the grand jury was still in session and was issuing subpoenas for testimony regarding the bombings — among those on the list: Bowling Green Mayor Robert Graham and four recently elected city commissioners.

Sources also confirmed that there was one, publicly unnamed, man who could likely shed light on the bombings. The man had reportedly told police he had been offered money to blow up the Cardinal Billiards pool room and was the individual who had "found" an unexploded bomb at another local business.

Another unnamed investigator admitted the probe into earlier bombings was stymied by the still unsolved murder of Graham. His brutal killing had not only eliminated a key witness but sent a sobering warning to anyone who was thinking of cooperating with police or a grand jury.

The anonymous member of law enforcement told a reporter, "We've got the worst bunch of hoodlums ever assembled around here at the present time. They used to be divided up into their own little groups, but now they've all gotten together and it could be really rough."

The news of the renewed grand jury probe was likely welcomed news for a group of local citizens who were part of a citizens committee convened by the previous mayor.

The group issued a report that said, "The menacing underworld tactics threatening our city must no longer be tolerated. Bowling Green must not become a terror-stricken city."

The public news that the grand jury was meeting about the bombings forced it to take extra security measures — changing meeting locations and ushering witnesses in through back doors guarded by police.

Along with the city officials, numerous law enforcement officials appeared in front of the grand jury, as did some unnamed "underworld" figures. At the end of the month, Judge Robert Coleman extended the grand jury's session until April; he took the opportunity to criticize the news stories about the grand jury's work, saying they made the jury's work even more difficult.

Whatever the obstacles, they again proved insurmountable as the grand jury quietly ended its term that summer with no indictments,

While the bombings remained unsolved, prosecutors were increasingly targeting the growing use of marijuana, especially among local college students. In one case, a Western student was sentenced to a year in jail for possessing what police labeled the "drug" of marijuana.

In response, a publication began circulating around town and the campus titled "*The Plain Brown Wrapper*."

The anonymously produced publication targeted racism in the city and also noted that while the high-profile bombings and several murders remained unsolved, law enforcement resources were being focused on marijuana use. In an article subtitled "How Lowe Can You Go," the writer(s) claimed Commonwealth's Attorney Lowe was using the marijuana busts to aid his reelection effort.

But bombings again took center stage in July when a bomb made up of several sticks of dynamite exploded at the Black Mt. Hebrew Presbyterian Church six miles north of the city. The church was empty when the blast went off, but the building sustained considerable damage.

Sheriff Watts downplayed the possibility that the bombing was racially motivated; Black leaders obviously disagreed, noting that while race relations in the city were generally better than in much of the country, no other motive made sense.

One Black leader told the *Daily News*, "I feel some outside agitators have come into the community in an attempt to stir up friction."

A day later, the FBI joined the bombing investigation, apparently under the theory that the bombing could be linked to other attacks on Black churches across the country at the time. Days later, another grand jury ended its terms without any indictments related to the bombings. As for the church attack, the grand jury blamed "outside agitators" seeking to "create an uneasiness in our country."

That summer, it seemed more cars than fish were being pulled from area rivers. In one week, five cars were pulled from Green River. They had been stolen from as far away as Ohio and apparently brought to Bowling Green to be stripped of the more valuable parts before being dumped.

Despite the many unsolved violent crimes on the books in Bowling Green, in November, Mayor R.D. Graham ordered police to focus on numerous other violators of law in the city — businesses that were open on Sundays. Kentucky, like some other states, had so-called "blue laws" that banned most businesses from opening on Sundays. (Why they were called "blue" laws is anyone's guess). The city had a similar law.

Graham issued a statement that said in part, "We cannot permit Bowling Green, known for its churches and schools, to become the first and only city in Kentucky running wide open on Sunday … a day set aside for worship and rest."

Sure enough, city police that next Sunday arrested 16 men, mostly owners of small stores, on charges that they violated the Sunday closing law. The issue became entangled in controversy, more arrests and legal challenges until most blue laws were eventually found by courts to be invalid or they were repealed.

It was a time of general turmoil in the city, with some city commissioners calling for the firing of the city manager over disagreements about his governing style, calls for police reform in light of the crime wave, and lawsuits over alleged mismanagement of the county school system. This was also joined by regular robberies, assaults, major fires, the now familiar bombings and other crimes.

Some hard numbers put the Bowling Green crime situation in clearer context in March of 1969.

The Kentucky Commission on Crime and Violence issued a first-of-its-kind report that found the crime rate in Bowling Green for the year of 1967 was about 47 percent higher than in similar-sized cities across the country. In six of seven crime categories studied, Bowling Green surpassed the national average. While the national homicide rate was 3.5 per 100,000 population, in Bowling Green the rate was 11.1 per 100,000. The city also had higher rates of rape, assault, burglary, larceny, and auto theft.

Various theories were offered for why crime was so high in the city, including the fact that Bowling Green was surrounded by a vast sea of "dry" counties — the only place between Louisville and Nashville where one could, legally, buy alcohol and thus a magnet for hard drinkers.

"The nuisance value of intoxication in Bowling Green is indicated by the fact that 46 per cent of the total arrests in 1967 were for drunken or related offenses," according to the report.

The report also painted a picture of ineffective policing, noting that the Bowling Green Police Department reported it had only solved 17 percent of major crimes in 1967, well below the national average. And even the 17 percent figure "is probably inflated," the report noted without explanation.

Not surprisingly, police and court officials were quick to attack the report.

"You can't stick your head in the sand and say Bowling Green is the best of cities, but (it) is not as bad as the report shows," said Police Court Judge George Boston.

Officials said the crime rate may have spiked in 1967 but had gone down by 1968 and into that year.

But in the waning days of 1969, there was one of the more high-profile bombings in the region's history.

Bowling Green residents for miles around were awakened by a terrific boom as the transmission tower for local television station WLTV was toppled by an estimated 48 sticks of dynamite. The 600-foot tower was in a remote section of the county, but the blast was heard for miles around. The destroyed equipment took the station off the air for almost two weeks.

Police logically assumed that the blast could have been retaliation for editorials and news stories the station had done about the recent crime wave. Like most of the bombings of that era, it would remain unsolved.

That fall, another grand jury tasked with examining lawlessness in the community cited a seeming lack of cooperation between law enforcement agencies as being an impediment to prosecutions.

Just days later, a new group called the Barren River Crime Council issued a report warning that it appeared that local criminals "perhaps with outside alliances," were increasingly organizing their business of the theft and resale of cars, livestock and farm equipment, as well as drug trafficking and other crimes.

The council also (although in couched language) put partial blame for the situation on inefficient courts and law enforcement, as well as what it deemed to be public apathy. Police, the council noted, were understaffed and inadequately trained.

As Bowling Green recovered from another heavy coating of snow and below-zero temperatures in the first days of the new year of 1970, Police Chief Constant released a report showing that city police had made 5,660 arrests in 1968; in 1969, that number spiked to 9,334. Constant said the increased number was a result of better policing and a spike in crime that was also being seen nationally.

As if in cue, that weekend, a pair of separate shootings in the city left two dead. Weeks later police raided two Bowling Green bars which were serving as fronts for illegal gun sales. Dozens of guns were seized, including a machine gun. Seemingly normal businesses were often being used for a range of illegal activity, from drug and gun sales to underage drinking and gambling.

One establishment that drew the scrutiny of law enforcement was called "The Nickel Bag." It was labeled as a "coffee house," and was owned by a 21-year-old Western student named Tom Crumbaker. Police said they had received numerous complaints about the business. The grand jury called Crumbaker to testify about the goings-on at what the *Daily News* called a "psychedelic" establishment.

Crumbaker denied there were any "subversive" activities at the Nickel and said it was a simple college student hangout.

The culture war nationally was also seen in Bowling Green. The same week of Crumbaker's testimony, the city commission adopted a resolution calling for the formation of a committee that would meet with theater owners and discourage them from showing "X" rated movies. The move came at a meeting packed with more than 100 community members, most in support of the effort. Proponents of the move had sent more than 400 letters to city officials.

Throughout that year, several murders made front-page news, but most were the result of domestic troubles or other squabbles not associated with the organized criminal activities.

In March, a grand jury said the only justified complaint against The Nickel Bag was that the bands playing there produced too much noise; the jury also jumped on the X-rated movie fray, saying that such movies needed more regulation.

Later that month, a passer-by saw a body floating face up in the Barren River in a rural part of the county called McFarland's Beach. When the body was pulled from the river by police, it was found to have been riddled with bullets.

The body, stripped clean of identification, was that of a young man, perhaps 18-20 years old. A further examination determined he had been shot five or six times, mostly at close range. The body was decomposed, indicating it had been in the river for a week or longer.

The only clue to the man's identity were two "homemade" rings on his fingers. Despite extensive news coverage and inquiries to police throughout the region, police were still stumped as to the man's identity days later.

A week later, the unclaimed body caused another issue — "I'd like to get rid of it," a hospital administrator told a reporter frankly as the body lay in the hospital's morgue. The unembalmed body was starting to "cause a little odor."

At the same time, police reported a possible break — several witnesses described having seen a man matching the victim's description in Bowling Green in the days before the killing. But the police only had a first name – Cliff.

While police investigated the mystery of the body in the river that April, a "dapper" Bowling Green gambler was charged with murder — for the fourth time.

Chapter 12

THE GAMBLER AND THE MURDERS

On April 7, 1970, the "King" was dethroned.

Clay Edward Ross, 46, was known around Bowling Green, for now unknown reasons, as "King" Ross.

On this spring night, he had a score to settle. He entered the Peppermint Lounge, a long-gone bar at Sixth and Kentucky Streets with an unsavory reputation, with a .22-caliber pistol in his pocket. Ross had been fired from his bartending job at the bar earlier that day.

Waiting for him was the bar's manager, Marion Parker Duke.

Duke, a 5-foot-6, gray-haired 64-year-old, was an unimposing presence. But as Ross was about to find out, Duke was anything but an easy target.

In his younger days, the "dapper" Duke was a gambler, nightspot operator — likely with mob ties — and daring criminal who was not above posing as a police officer to commit armed robberies.

So, when Duke saw Ross, he pulled out his own gun — a .25-caliber pistol. A shootout followed.

In the end, Ross was dead, and Duke and a bar patron had non-fatal bullet wounds.

Duke was arrested and charged with murder.

The incident was front-page news, but it was nothing compared to 1952. That year, Duke was charged with a triple slaying that the *Daily News* reported was "as brutal and savage a homicide as ever committed in Warren County."

What followed were numerous court battles featuring well-known Kentucky figures, followed by allegations of police corruption that also made statewide headlines.

Not much is known about Duke's early years, other than he was born on October 22, 1905, in Paducah, Kentucky. He moved around often, living (when he wasn't in jail) in various locations in Kentucky and, for a time, in Nashville.

When Duke's activities are traceable, it's because he was in the news for a series of criminal activities.

In 1942, the *Courier-Journal* reported he was arrested on charges of grand larceny in Louisville for allegedly stealing $900 from a car. Three years later, he was accused of stealing 12 cases of whiskey from a warehouse.

A year later, he was in Nashville, charged with receiving and concealing stolen property.

One of his most noteworthy criminal capers came in 1950 in Nashville.

Duke, who was described at the time as a "light-skinned" Black man who sometimes was mistaken as being white, entered the New Era club in Nashville, along with two accomplices. The trio claimed they were police officers.

Once inside, the three men tied up four employees and broke into the club's safe, getting away with $860. Duke was arrested a few weeks later in Indiana and was extradited to Tennessee.

Police told the *Tennessean* newspaper that they planned to interview Duke in connection to a rash of similar crimes, including an "alleged $5,000 mystery holdup of another Negro nightspot. The latter robbery is alleged to have occurred during the World Series in 1949 and remained unreported for several weeks. It was understood threats had been made on the lives of the owners if the robbery was reported to police."

It's unknown how much time Duke spent behind bars, but by 1952 he was living part-time in Bowling Green, at a rooming house in the 300 block of Chestnut Street.

He was reportedly then a manager of a nightspot in Kentucky's "Sin City" — Newport. It's not known exactly how Duke fit within the web of corruption in Newport, but his work there would have come under the umbrella of the mobsters running the city's nightspots.

The career criminal seemed to never have a shortage of funds at the time — he reportedly had a trunk with $6,000 cash in it (equivalent today to about $70,000), and once he was lodged in the Warren County Jail, he was known for having pricey rabbit and chicken dinners delivered to him and other inmates from local restaurants.

The boarding house in the Shake Rag area of Bowling Green where Duke had a room was owned by Narcissus Bell, 67. Also living in the eight-room house were Bell's sister, Josephine Abernathy, 65, and a tenant, Horace Buford, 26.

Bell was the widow of an L&N Railroad employee, Sherman Bell. Buford worked at the Mayhugh and McReynolds Garage on Louisville Road.

On September 25, a Thursday, Duke called Bowling Green police. He told them he had returned from a trip to Newport on Wednesday night but found the doors to the Chestnut Street home locked, with no one answering his knocks. He returned several more times, to no avail, he said, so he went and spent the night in Franklin with friends.

On Thursday, Duke said, he returned and asked neighbors if they had seen anyone at the home. When they replied that they hadn't, Duke and another man opened a window and Duke entered.

Inside the ransacked house were the bloodied and battered bodies of Bell, Abernathy and Buford.

The first policeman on the scene was soon joined by Coroner Raymond McClard, Bowling Green Police Chief Murrell Waddle and Capt. Hubert Phelps. The men had to step carefully over pools of blood and household items scattered throughout the house.

McClard reported that Buford had been shot six times — five times in the head and once in the shoulder — apparently while he lay in his bed.

The coroner concluded Bell and Abernathy had been beaten to death, and then both bodies shot twice. Their bodies were in a bedroom of the house, which had been thoroughly ransacked.

Based on empty shells, Waddle determined two guns had been used in the shooting — a .38-caliber automatic and a .38-caliber "Special."

The house, the *Daily News* reported, was usually tidy but today "was left in a shambles. … Even the door housing the refrigerator motor had been ripped off."

But in the back of the house, an undisturbed table still had a pair of dice and a few coins on it.

It appeared that the women had been engaged in a "terrific struggle."

Suspicion soon landed on Duke, the man with the lengthy rap sheet.

He was taken to police headquarters and interrogated, where he denied any knowledge of the killings.

But the trail of evidence was working against Duke. In the room Duke occupied, police found a pair of his shoes with blood on them stuffed in a suitcase.

Another break then came when Garnett Butts and Roy "Shorty" Edwards, employees at the Dixie Garage, saw a bag floating in the Barren River under the College Street Bridge.

Inside, police found a .38-caliber Special and a pair of pliers. Duke admitted he had owned a similar bag but said it had gone missing from his room "for some time."

Duke was arrested the next day and charged with three counts of murder. He was taken to the Warren County Jail and relieved of almost $300 in cash and a knife he was carrying.

The task of prosecuting Duke fell to William H. Natcher. Natcher would soon go on to represent Kentucky in the U.S. House of Representatives for a record 41 years.

Duke, meanwhile, retained the services of the best-known lawyer in town, Rodes K. Myers. The brilliant and often flamboyant Myers served as lieutenant governor from 1939 to 1943 and had a national reputation for his involvement in many high-profile cases.

Among his other clients was notorious brothel-keeper Pauline Tabor, who was able to keep her lucrative business open for decades despite frequent attempts, by Natcher and others, to close it down.

Despite being on opposite sides of the courtroom in many high-profile cases, Natcher and Myers were close social friends and united in their involvement in Democratic Party politics.

As he awaited arraignment, Duke gave an interview to the *Daily News* in which he restated his innocence. He said he had brought two friends from Louisville to get rooms at the house Wednesday, but after a bout of heavy drinking that night, they returned to the house to find the doors locked with no one answering his knocks. He then returned several times Thursday before finding the bodies.

The two men with Duke, Richard Clifford Woods and Taylor L. Slaughter, had in the meantime been found in Barren County, and after police found two revolvers and a sawed-off shotgun in their car, charged with carrying concealed weapons. The men, who also had criminal records, were brought to Bowling Green to face questioning.

Waddle presented his theory of the case to the *Daily News*: Duke and the two men (along with some female companions) had returned to the house around midnight. When Bell said Woods and Slaughter could not spend the night in her home, Duke "flew into a drunken rage" and killed the three residents.

He then changed clothes, leaving behind the bloody shoes, and ransacked the house to make it look like a robbery, Waddle theorized. Duke then threw the bag with the gun in it into the Barren River.

Waddle added that Duke had told him the nightspot in Newport he worked in allowed gambling, and he used to be a card dealer there before rising in the ranks to be a manager of the establishment.

While Duke was in the Warren County Jail, he reportedly regularly had expensive meals brought in for himself and other inmates. Food was reportedly at the heart of a jail incident involving Duke and another inmate, who was attempting to get extra food from the jail trustees. The disagreement became physical, and Duke slashed the other inmate with a knife, which he later said he had "found" in the jail. The inmate was stitched up and returned to jail, while Duke's punishment was to be sent to a different cell.

Natcher announced in January he would seek the death penalty for Duke. The *Daily News* reported that the last execution from a Warren County case was in the 1890s and took place by hanging.

As was common at the time, Duke was to be tried separately for each alleged murder, with the prosecution first trying the case of Bell's killing.

Myers, meanwhile, asked the court that the victims' bodies be exhumed so further ballistic tests could be conducted and the bodies autopsied. The court agreed, and the bodies of the sisters were scheduled to be exhumed from the Mount Mariah Cemetery and Buford's body was to be exhumed from a Glasgow cemetery.

On March 12, the process began. Overseeing it was BGPD Captain Phelps, who told reporters no bullets, only fragments, were retrieved from the bodies. Dr. Richard Grise conducted autopsies on all three victims, who were then reburied the next day.

As the trial approached, Judge John B. Rodes ordered an extra 100 potential jurors be called to supplement the 30 already called to serve on juries. The larger pool was needed because potential jurors would be excluded if they opposed capital punishment.

In April, Rodes drew 101 names of potential jurors. The pool included "at least" two Black members and one woman. The non-all-White male makeup of potential jurors was unusual enough at the time to be mentioned in newspaper articles.

On April 20, jury selection began at the Warren County Courthouse.

Duke, looking dapper in a light-colored suit with a handkerchief in his jacket pocket, stopped to be photographed on the steps of the Warren County Jail as he prepared for the short trip to the courthouse. In the picture, Duke shares a laugh with Myers, and the *Daily News* reported the accused "appeared in a jovial mood."

The jury selection process in a packed courtroom took almost four hours as 26 potential jurors, including the only four women in the jury pool, were disqualified for saying they had already formed an opinion on the case. Eight potential jurors were excused for saying they opposed the death penalty, and one potential juror was dismissed because he had a hearing problem.

The jury was all White, with Myers using one of his challenges to exclude the one Black member of the jury pool.

Testimony in the trial began the next day, where the basic facts of the case were laid out.

Natcher told jurors that Duke flew into a drunken rage after being told his friends could not stay in the house and then committed the murders.

Ann Oldham, a 33-year-old Bowling Green woman, was a key witness for the prosecution, as she detailed the night before the killings.

Oldham said she was called from Louisville by Woods, asking her for a "date" (the word was repeatedly used in quotations in newspaper articles of the time). Woods and Slaughter met her at the Morocco Club, where she worked, at Third and Chestnut Streets in Bowling Green.

A few hours later, the trio went across the street to the Mustang Inn to also get Slaughter a companion for the night.

Duke, with fat rolls of cash stuffed in his pockets, walked into the Mustang Inn accompanied by two women. The group drank beer and whiskey for several hours before heading to the Elks Club for more drinking. Finally, around midnight, Duke, Slaughter, Woods, Oldham and another woman went to the Chestnut Street boarding house.

According to Oldham, Abernathy told Duke the two couples could not spend the night there, and urged him to go to bed.

Duke, Oldham testified, was visibly drunk and raising his voice.

He finally yelled out, "If my friends can't stay, I won't either," according to Oldham.

The two couples decided to leave, but before they did, Duke retrieved a "pickle jar" from his room filled with "silver and a roll of currency" to show the couples.

When the two couples left minutes later, Duke stayed behind, Oldham testified. Others in the drinking party that night told essentially the same story.

A Yellow Cab driver testified that a woman had called for a cab from the house shortly after midnight, but when he arrived at the home and blew his horn, no one came out. He said the shades were drawn but he could make out someone moving in the house.

Another cab driver, Ollie Meffert, testified that he picked up Duke about 3 a.m. at the L&N Depot and drove him to Franklin.

For the defense, Duke was his own star witness. Under Myers' careful questioning, Duke, described as "calm and self-assured," recounted his version of events.

Duke said he had returned the week of the killings from a gambling trip to Detroit and Gary, Indiana, with more than $6,000 in winnings. More than $4,800 in cash, wrapped in a pink towel, and a large amount of silver was in his trunk in the Chestnut Street home the night of the murders, he said.

Duke said he had told Bell about his good fortune that week and had given her some extra money to buy enough coal to last the winter.

On the night of the murders, Duke admitted to a long drinking spree with several women, along with Woods and Slaughter, before he returned to the home with the two couples. He said after the two couples left, he also left to visit a friend and fellow gambler, Lawrence "Pig Meat" Nichols. He then reiterated his story about not being able to get into the house until the next day. He added that the locker in his room had been opened, and the money and silver was gone.

As for the bloodstained shoes, Duke said he had not worn them in weeks.

Myers told jurors that the real culprits were after Duke's money, and they dipped his client's shoes in a pool of blood to frame him.

To bolster that claim, Myers called several witnesses to cast suspicion on others. One witness testified he had seen a man resembling an ex-con he knew loitering around the Chestnut Street home the day before the murders. The man was apparently still in a Georgia jail at the time of the murders, but Myers hinted that he had information that the man had escaped four days prior to the killings.

Also called was Dr. Grise, who had performed autopsies on the exhumed bodies. He testified that the victims had head fractures likely caused by a wide, blunt object. Myers pointed out that a brick was found in the car occupied by Woods and Slaughter when they were stopped.

The forensic evidence in the case was analyzed by two FBI special agents. Agent Robert M. Zimmer said the pistol found in the bag in the Barren River was one of the murder weapons. The other gun used was never located.

Agent Edwin Donaldson testified to finding human blood not only on the pair of Duke's shoes, but on a pair of his pajamas and the suitcase.

Under cross-examination by Myers, Donaldson said he had found no blood on any of Duke's other clothing, and he admitted that the shoes could have been placed in a pool of blood in an effort to frame his client.

In his closing arguments, Myers called Duke "an innocent man — a framed man," and had harsh words for local law enforcement, calling police chief Waddle "Chief of the local Gestapo."

Natcher claimed his friend Myers had resorted to a "centipede defense" to cast suspicion on numerous others.

The case ended after five days of packed courtrooms, with the *Daily News* calling it "one of the longest and most bitterly contested in Warren Circuit Court history."

The 12 jurors were given the case for deliberation at 7:30 p.m. on a Thursday night. The jurors dismissed at 10:13 p.m. and reconvened on Friday morning at 8:30 a.m. After three more hours, the jurors "showing signs of weariness" told Judge Rodes they could not reach a verdict. He ordered them to return for more deliberations, but just 30 minutes later, they returned to say they were hopelessly deadlocked, and Rodes declared a mistrial.

Duke smiled and shook Myers' hand. While Duke was spared a likely trip to the electric chair, Myers was perhaps almost equally pleased — he told reporters that he had handled 287 murder trials in his almost 30-year career, and never had a client sentenced to death.

Judge Rodes set Duke's bond at $10,500, but the state Department of Probation and Paroles later ruled that Duke was a parole violator based on a previous conviction in Jefferson County. As the issue was litigated in the court system, Duke remained in jail.

The second trial, slated to begin in November 1953, was delayed by Judge Rodes because it was "tobacco season," and most jurors were farmers who needed to be in their fields.

Finally, in January 1954, jury selection began for the second trial.

While Myers was still defending Duke, the prosecution now fell to new Commonwealth's Attorney Frank Goad. Natcher had in August been elected to his first term to Congress.

On January 19, the all-male, all-White jury began hearing testimony. The prosecution case was essentially the same as presented in the first trial. Oldham again described the night of drinking and Duke appearing to be upset that his friends weren't allowed to stay in the home.

To counter Myers' defense strategy to imply that others, notably Slaughter and Woods, were the killers, the prosecution called a gas station attendant to testify that he sold gas to the men at about 12:30 a.m. at the Lost River service station. This bolstered the men's claim that they were heading to Nashville after leaving Duke at the Chestnut Street home.

FBI agent Donaldson this time testified that Duke's bloodstained shoes could not have been a product of someone simply placing the shoes in blood. He said the blood was so saturated in the leather that they must have been worn during the bloodbath.

During the testimony, Duke "appeared alternately bored and amused ...," the *Daily News* reported. He frequently yawned, stretched and smiled.

Duke was again the main witness for his own defense.

On the stand, he said he had a very close relationship with the slain women.

"I respected those ladies. They treated me like I was a member of the family, and I treated them the same way."

Duke admitted he was "pretty well loaded" on the night of the murders but downplayed any disagreement about his friends staying the night at the home.

"There was not even a cross word," he said.

The jury began deliberations on a Friday morning, and a little less than two hours later, reported it had reached a verdict: guilty of manslaughter. The conviction carried a 21-year sentence.

Duke remained defiant when briefly interviewed by a *Daily News* reporter.

"Anybody who would do a thing like that deserves the electric chair. Me or anybody else, and I didn't do it," he said. "I think it was a rotten verdict, and it looks like a prejudiced jury was picked by the Commonwealth."

Myers had once again kept a client from execution, but Duke was destined to spend the better part of the next two decades at the state penitentiary in Eddyville.

Goad eventually decided to not pursue separate trials for the murders of the two other victims, and the Duke case appeared to be over.

But just months later, it would reappear in an unexpected way.

In March, Police Chief Waddle asked the city to fire the man who had been the department's lead investigator in many high-profile cases, Captain Phelps.

Waddle charged that Phelps had violated numerous department policies. While the formal charges were lengthy, the primary allegation boiled down to this: Phelps, Waddle charged, had been feeding information regarding the Duke police investigation to Myers.

The chief had apparently asked Phelps to resign when the allegations first surfaced, but when Phelps said he intended to keep working, Waddle brought the charges to city officials.

Phelps said the allegations were false and he intended to "fight it out ... take it to court if necessary."

In anticipation of a potential court battle, Phelps knew he needed the best lawyer in town. Not surprisingly, he hired Myers, despite the seeming conflict of interest.

A "jury" composed of members of the city's "Board of Councilmen and Board of Aldermen" heard two hours of testimony, behind closed doors, regarding Waddle's charges on March 17.

Twenty minutes after the hearing ended, the jury announced its finding that Phelps was guilty of all charges, and he was immediately fired.

Phelps soon fired back.

He charged in a complaint to city officials that Waddle himself engaged in a wide range of misconduct, including withholding evidence, undermining police department captains and protecting "gambling houses and houses of prostitution" in the city.

In terms of the Duke case, Phelps charged that Waddle had protected Woods, a key figure in the prosecution of Duke, from further investigations into crimes he may have committed. He added the charge that Waddle "knew Woods falsely testified," in Duke's trial.

Myers took the opportunity to issue a statement, admitting he had approached Phelps for information in the Duke case "because I knew him to be truthful ... Chief Waddle perhaps takes offense because this evidence was not concealed from the public, the court and the jury."

A week later, a three-hour hearing was held regarding the allegations. After just six minutes of deliberations, city officials voted 11-1 to clear Waddle, who remained police chief until 1959.

In 1969, Duke was released from Eddyville after serving almost 16 years.

Duke returned to Bowling Green and lived in the Downtown Hotel. He soon was running the Peppermint Lounge, a watering hole with a less than stellar reputation.

The establishment was the scene of a non-fatal 1969 shooting. The victim declined to tell police who had shot him. A year later, a man was found dead in the bar, slumped in a chair. The man's death was later ruled to be due to natural causes.

The official owner of the bar was another Downtown Hotel resident named Ebon Ray Green. At the time of the Ross shooting, however, Green was under indictment for allegedly shooting and killing his common-law wife. Duke claimed he was purchasing the business from Green.

The numerous deaths associated with the bar and the people running it led the *Daily News* to editorialize that "there may be some reasonable explanation for the licensing and inspection procedures that have permitted a tavern at Sixth and Kentucky Streets ... to operate as it has, but if there is, a lot of Bowling Green citizens probably would be interested in hearing it."

Ross, a resident of Fourth Street, worked at the bar. Ross also had numerous brushes with the law, having been charged with carrying a concealed weapon, shooting and killing a dog and attempted murder after attacking a man during a baseball game at the Warren County Fairgrounds.

Duke had fired Ross, for allegedly stealing money from the business, the morning of the shooting.

That night, Duke was in the bar with one patron, a man named Excell Jenkins.

When Ross walked into the bar, Duke said to Jenkins, "Oh Lord, here comes trouble."

Duke told Ross to leave, and the man seemed to be complying, turning to go out the door. But at that point, Ross spun around, pulled a pistol from his pocket and began shooting.

Duke pulled out his gun and returned fire. While both Duke and Jenkins had been shot once and suffered minor injuries, Ross had been hit "five or six times," Coroner J.C. Kirby later reported.

At a preliminary hearing, Duke's attorney, Robert Simons, argued that his client had acted in self-defense. But Warren County Judge Basil Griffin sent the case to a grand jury.

The grand jury indicted Duke on a charge of carrying a concealed deadly weapon, but declined to indict him on the murder charge, apparently believing he had acted in self-defense. Duke pleaded guilty to the weapons charge and paid a $25 fine plus court costs.

In June, Duke placed a legal advertisement in the *Daily News* signaling his intent to apply for a liquor license with the state to operate at the Peppermint Lounge location.

The business was to be renamed "Duke's Cafe."

But the cafe never materialized with Duke's death a year later, at the age of 65.

Unlike his chaotic life, Duke passed quietly — his death failed to even garner a mention in the newspapers that had reported exhaustively on the gambler's various exploits.

Chapter 13

THE FEDS STEP IN

As police continued to search for the identity of the young man found floating in the Barren River in 1970, the city was hit with an unwelcome designation. Bowling Green was in a federal program called Model Cities, which aimed to fight poverty and promote renewal efforts in cities across the country.

That year, the Justice Department labeled Bowling Green as being one of the country's "Model Cities" with an "urgent crime problem." While that designation meant the city could get federal funds for policing efforts, it was obviously not a description welcomed by city officials.

In response, Mayor R.D. Graham said Bowling Green's crime problem was no worse than anywhere else.

The coming months, however, would challenge the mayor's assertion.

In late April, the body in the river was identified as being that of an 18-year-old New York state man named Clifford Reardon. He was in the Marine Corps stationed in North Carolina, and the identification was made through military dental records.

Just days later, a Marine who had gone AWOL, Jerry Wayne Jackson, was arrested in Indiana and charged with Reardon's murder. Jackson, a former Bowling Green resident, had apparently left Camp LeJeune in North Carolina at the same time as Reardon. Jackson later pleaded guilty to manslaughter and was sentenced to serve 20 years.

Some sobering crime statistics were released that summer. The Barren River Regional Crime Council reported that crime was on pace to increase almost 100 percent for the year. The report noted there were 10 homicides in Warren County in just the first three months of 1970, and the local crime rate in just about every category was significantly higher than the national average. As if it were any consolation, the council determined the crimes were being perpetrated by unconnected locals.

"No evidence was uncovered of gang or Mafia-type crime," according to the report.

The Council went public later that summer with a multi-step proposal to fight crime. The plan included streamlining local court processes, better training for law enforcement, and targeting crimes committed by juveniles.

These headline-grabbing stories would later be the basis for claims that Bowling Green had the highest per-capita murder rate in the country at the time. While that exact claim to infamy may be questionable, there was no doubt that the city was a hotbed for criminal activity.

As if on cue, the same week that the *Daily News* was writing about the crime report, a Bowling Green bar called The Pub was blown up by a dynamite bomb. The owner of the bar escaped with only a minor scratch, despite the power of a blast that was heard 10 blocks away.

When police asked the owner of the bar if he knew of anyone who had a motive to destroy the bar, they heard a familiar answer: no.

Meanwhile, it seemed police were pulling out as many bodies from the Barren River as anglers were reeling in bass and crappie.

The day after the explosion at The Pub, the body of a 57-year-old Bowling Green man was pulled from the river. The man had been stabbed and badly beaten. The man was quickly identified as a 57-year-old named William Morrow. Unlike many other murder cases, police made a quick arrest. An informant told police he saw three men rob Morrow and stab him before dumping him in the watery grave. The men had gotten 90 cents, and two cigarettes, from Morrow in the robbery. The three men were quickly rounded up and charged with murder.

Days later, firefighters responded to a house fire on 2nd Street early on a Saturday morning. After the blaze was extinguished, firefighters noticed a strange pile of charred newspapers and magazines. Underneath was the body of 76-year-old Eva McDaniels. A cursory exam showed she had been hit in the head with a blunt object — likely a hammer or piece of metal pipe. Her death was ruled a homicide, with the fire an obvious attempt to hide any evidence.

A witness had reported seeing several people leaving McDaniels' house around the time of the blaze. Based on that testimony, a

27-year-old carpenter, William Hughie Glass, was arrested in connection to the crime the next day. Adding to the litany of crimes that year was a fatal shooting at Beech Bend Park that left a Hart County man dead; his girlfriend was charged with murder.

The killings and bombings had the community on edge. There was likely little consolation in that the bombings that plagued Bowling Green were not unique. That summer, Sen. John McLellan of Arkansas announced he was starting an investigation into the more than 5,000 bombings that had occurred across the country in the last 18 months.

McLellan called the bombings "a rebellion against society."

Whatever the cause, the bombings spurred calls for new federal regulations regarding the sale and handling of dynamite and nitroglycerin.

McLellan eventually pushed through federal legislation called the Organized Crime Control Act later that year.

Its provisions included the creation of special grand juries, immunity for witnesses, making illegal gambling a federal crime, and repealing the outdated 1917 federal law regarding explosives that made them readily available.

The biggest impact of the Organized Crime Control Act, however, came with the establishment of federal legislation regarding "Racketeer Influenced and Corrupt Organizations."

The so-called RICO law, still used to this day, allowed the federal prosecution of groups engaged in illegal activity. It was first widely used to prosecute the Mafia but subsequently has been used to go after other groups.

A tool to go after organized crime operations, like a car theft ring that would soon make headlines, was sorely needed.

Chapter 14

THE CHRISTMAS TREE

Darrell Moody was punctual.

The men who planned to kill Moody, a detective captain in the Bowling Green Police Department, were counting on it.

His wife, Betty Moody, had left their small brick home on Henry Avenue on the morning of February 16, 1972, at her usual time around 8 a.m. She was headed to her waitress job at Ray's Drive In on the U.S. 31-W Bypass, while her 9-year-old daughter was walking to T.C. Cherry Elementary School a block away.

Normally, Darrell Moody would have been still at home alone at 8:30 that morning before he had to leave for work at the Bowling Green Police Department around 9 a.m. But he had a court appearance that morning, so he got into his car around 8:32 a.m.

As he was turning the key in his Oldsmobile's ignition, a thunderous blast that was heard blocks away shattered the quiet neighborhood.

Bricks, splinters of charred wood, shards of glass and pieces of furniture littered the lawn, and the walls and ceilings of homes across the street were cracked by the blast.

Darrell Moody was shaken, but uninjured, as he called police headquarters on his car radio.

As firefighters and law enforcement officials swarmed the scene, they smelled a familiar odor — the heavy, sweet smell of dynamite.

It was a familiar odor at crime scenes in the city in recent years. The veteran police officer Moody had undoubtedly made many enemies among the men and women he had locked up over his career, so the list of bombing suspects could be lengthy.

But at the time, Moody was closing in on the massive car theft ring that had emerged in Bowling Green in recent years.

By 1972, the ring had spread to 10 states, but it was no secret that Moody was working with the FBI and other law enforcement agencies to dismantle it.

For the group's leaders, the solution seemed simple: Blow up Moody's house, with him inside.

❖❖❖❖❖

The car theft ring got its start in Bowling Green, apparently with the discovery that some makes of cars were especially convenient targets for theft and resale.

"Volkswagens were popular to steal because the (vehicle identification number) was easy to change, and then they could register them," former Bowling Green police Chief Gary Raymer said years later. As the demand increased, the ring "began taking orders (for any particular type of stolen car). People jumped at that."

A house on Old Iron Bridge Road west of Bowling Green was used as the location to alter the VIN numbers and process the stolen cars. As the business grew, the operation moved nearby to a former service station on Porter Pike. License plates were thrown in a pond near Lovers Lane on the outskirts of the city. As the ring got more adept at falsifying bills of sale and other papers, it started selling the cars to dealers as well as individuals.

Moody was soon on its trail, and he proved to be a formidable foe.

Joe Denning, a former BGPD officer and Kentucky State Police trooper, said Moody "was one of the best investigators I've ever known."

The sentiment was echoed by former Bowling Green police officer Jim Rogers, who said Moody had a photographic memory and was a tireless investigator who regularly had FBI agents and other law enforcement officials waiting at his office door to get information.

Gary Lusher, who served in various capacities with KSP from 1970 to 1994, said Moody was "a bulldog. He wouldn't turn loose ... and he was a very intelligent investigator."

"His major goal was to wipe out that car theft ring," Rogers said.

Those efforts put a target on Moody's back.

The late 1960s and early 1970s were a generally dangerous time for law enforcement.

Police officers "walked a beat with no car, no radio to call in backup," Raymer recalled. "You had a nightstick, gun and handcuffs," and, if you were lucky, "the goodwill of the people."

"There was a lot of anti-police sentiment at the time," recalled Tommy Loving, a former KSP trooper and later head of the Bowling Green-Warren County Drug Task Force.

Around that time, the bootlegging, gambling and car theft enterprises had been joined by drug dealing, often based out of truck stops. The same roads that served as the highways for drug trafficking were soon also filled with stolen vehicles making their way to and from Bowling Green.

As arrests in the car theft operation appeared imminent, the leaders of the group "decided to have (Moody) killed," Raymer said.

Rogers was a close friend of Moody's. He recalls that on the night of February 15, 1972, Moody's brick bungalow on Henry Avenue was filled with police officers who were discussing reviving a local Fraternal Order of Police lodge.

Apparently, at some point that night or early the next morning, a bomb made of several sticks of dynamite was placed in the crawlspace under the Moody home.

"Moody was a creature of habit – he never left home till 9 a.m.," Rogers said. But as fate would have it, Moody had the court appearance that day.

"When he got in the car and turned the key, the house exploded," Rogers said.

The bomb had apparently been set off by a remote-control device.

"I had just turned the key, and I thought. 'There goes my car,'" Moody told the *Daily News* in a 1984 interview. "But then I thought, 'No, because I'm still here.'"

Rogers was among those who rushed to the scene.

"The house was just sticks," he recalled.

Moody said he saw the house rise from its foundation from the force of the blast.

The destroyed house was never rebuilt, leaving a lot that remains vacant in the middle of a quiet Bowling Green street.

Despite the lengthy history of bombings in Bowling Green, the attack on Moody "got everyone's attention," Loving said.

Police quickly zeroed in on two men tied to the car theft operation as being responsible for the bombing, and they were indicted that day. Neither man made it to court.

One of the men, Melvin Eugene Moore, allegedly had raped a woman that same day and was making his escape on a highway near London, Kentucky, when he was stopped by a state trooper. Moore shot and wounded the trooper and was putting him in the trunk of his cruiser when another trooper arrived on the scene and shot and killed Moore.

The other man indicted was Kenneth Wayne Taylor, who was still being sought by police when he was shot and killed later that year by another man with a criminal record.

Despite the attempt on his life, Moody was not the kind of investigator who would be scared off a case.

Moody had started walking a beat as a Bowling Green police officer in 1955. His salary was $2,748 per year for a job that was notoriously dangerous.

"You didn't have any backup," Moody told the *Daily News* in the 1984 interview. "You either whipped the other guy or got whipped. And I've gotten whipped a few times."

One of Darrell Moody's two sons from his first marriage, Kelly Moody, said his father only talked about his career — including his brushes with death — when Kelly Moody was older.

Kelly Moody said his father had also once been shot in the stomach while policing.

"They tried to do everything to him," Kelly Moody said.

Despite the violence around him, those who knew Darrell Moody described him as a warm and humorous person outside his law enforcement activities.

Kelly Moody said they would be having lunch at the former Murray's restaurant in Bowling Green "and people would come up and say, 'Thank you for arresting me. You changed my life.'"

"He could be a silly, happy-go-lucky guy," Kelly Moody said.

Family pictures show him dressed as a Keystone Kop, and Kelly Moody said his father had purchased a garish orange blazer at a thrift shop and made sure to wear it whenever he was scheduled to be on television.

"That was his interview jacket," Kelly Moody said.

Hillary Hightower is Darrell Moody's niece.

"He was funny, smart ... and a really good detective," she said. He told her stories about the threats and attacks but indicated "he would not have traded any of it."

After the bombing of their house, the Moodys moved to a home on Magnolia Street, where that December they decorated the house for Christmas.

The car theft ring operators got word to Darrell Moody that if he took his Christmas tree down, they would make good on their efforts to kill him, Kelly Moody said.

"They were trying to make him look foolish," he said.

But Darrell Moody turned the threat into a challenge and decided to keep the tree up until the ringleaders were behind bars.

He said, "We'll just celebrate Christmas all year long," Kelly Moody recalled. "It was right in the window, lit up," he said.

"He left that tree up for some time," Lusher said. "He wasn't one to give up."

What few people knew, aside from Moody, was that the effort to destroy the car theft ring was already irrevocably in motion at the time of the bombing.

That summer, there were whispers around town that the investigation was coming to a conclusion. The rumors took concrete form when people saw law enforcement officers supervising the drainage of the large pond off Cemetery Road near the intersection with Scottsville Road and Cumberland Trace. A fire truck was pumping a reported 500 pounds of water a minute out of the pond. Police confirmed they were looking for evidence related to car thefts.

Finally, based largely on Moody's work that spanned several years, 41 people were indicted in August 1972 by a federal grand jury on charges related to operating the car theft ring. Seventeen were from Warren County, while others were from Louisville and other parts of the state.

Moody and the Bowling Green police department had been aided by law enforcement from 10 states, the FBI, and Kentucky State Police in the investigation. The indictments, which were formally unveiled in Washington, D.C., included 28 people who were allegedly stealing the cars and 13 others who were involved in the effort to sell the cars.

According to the indictments, the ringleaders were conspiring to kill other witnesses as law enforcement closed in on them.

There was grand jury testimony that three witnesses had cash bounties put on their lives.

Two of the defendants had reportedly discussed killing a witness in the very federal courthouse where the grand jury was meeting.

One of the men indicted in the car theft ring was Kenneth Wayne Taylor, who had also been indicted in the Moody bombing and was still at large. Another indictment was handed down for Melvin Eugene Moore, the other alleged bomber of the Moody house, despite the fact that he had been killed months earlier.

After weeks of legal maneuvers, a federal judge in Bowling Green ruled that 25 of the defendants would face a single trial.

U.S. District Attorney C. Fred Partin was leading the prosecution. He asked a judge to move the trial to Louisville. Publicly, he said the reason for the request was two-fold: pre-trial publicity could taint the local jury pool; and he said there were not enough local hotel rooms for the staggering 600 witnesses he expected to call. Partin said he discovered Bowling Green had only 547 hotel rooms, with about half available at any time.

While those were the stated reasons for the request, it is likely Partin was concerned that a local jury would be sympathetic to, or scared of, the local defendants.

He alluded to that issue when he said in a hearing that Bowling Green is "a tightly knit community."

Judge Mac Swinford, however, ruled that the trial would stay in Bowling Green, saying that traveling 100 miles or so to Louisville for the trial would be an unfair burden on the defendants.

The trial was expected to take up to two months, during which, Swinford ruled, the jury would remain sequestered.

The massive trial, now with a witness list approaching 1,000 people, was expected to likely be the longest in Kentucky history and cost around $800,000 – almost $6 million in 2025 dollars. Most of the cost was to house witnesses in local hotels.

The federal government also rented the Capitol Theater in downtown Bowling Green to hold witnesses as they prepared to testify at the nearby courthouse.

Ultimately, 25 people were slated to face trial in U.S. District Court in Bowling Green in April 1973.

The first task was to select a jury. Judge Swinford told prospective jurors, as well as the attorneys for the defendants, that jury tampering was a concern, based on other cases where jurors had been contacted in an effort to sway their vote.

The potential for unwanted contact was also on the mind of many prospective jurors, who asked to be removed from the jury pool. A few jurors were also tentatively approved to serve, only to have their names removed, without a publicly stated reason given, the next day. It seems likely the court received some information about the jurors' ties to defendants.

It took several days, but finally a jury of 12 and six alternates were selected from a pool of 300. The process was made more cumbersome because the defendants were being represented by six attorneys.

At one point, the attorneys could not agree on whether to accept or dismiss one of the potential jurors, and asked Swinford to step in. The judge said he couldn't mediate the dispute, so the attorneys said they had no choice but to accept the jury that had been selected.

The trial started with testimony from a pair of men who said defendants Billy Mayes and Nathan McDaniel recruited them to join a new car theft business in 1968.

The men said they would receive orders on what type of car to steal, with pay for the thefts ranging from $200 for a Volkswagen to $600 for a Cadillac. Some cars were stolen to be stripped of parts to be resold.

The men also testified that Mayes threatened that anyone who snitched would be dealt with harshly.

Mayes reportedly said he "could get anybody done in because he's got some real wild hippie friends."

Several other witnesses, who said they were part of the ring and who were testifying in exchange for immunity, continued to detail the thefts, estimating that more than 1,800 cars had been stolen. The operation also involved creating false registrations for the vehicles. The witnesses said the stolen cars would be left in various parking lots around the city to be picked up by Mayes.

Some of the cars with fake registrations were sold to unsuspecting buyers, while, according to testimony, many were sold to unscrupulous car dealers. Some were used in insurance fraud schemes. The local operators were also working with car theft operations in Indianapolis, Louisville and as far away as Chicago.

The testimony dragged on for weeks, with witness after witness detailing how they stole, purchased, or knew about stolen vehicles.

Moody was finally called to take the stand. He detailed his lengthy investigation and his more personal battle with the ring operators.

He was asked if he had taken a "blood oath" to keep his Christmas tree up. He said he hadn't, but the tree was still up, he admitted.

He was then asked if he had sent post cards to one of the defendants, Willie Hudson, in jail.

Some of the cards were described as "obscene;" another Christmas card had a picture of a jailed Hudson on it with "Ho Ho Hell" written on it.

Moody said he may have sent a card to Hudson, but claimed he was not responsible for the cards in question.

The humorous tone of the testimony was an outlier; just the next day, it was revealed that a witness had entered the courthouse with a gun. The man, who was described as a well-known Corvette thief, told officials he was afraid for his life as a result of testifying. The man, who lived in Louisville, had reportedly also brought a sawed-off shotgun and a submachine gun to Bowling Green.

As the trial entered its fourth week, both sides agreed that some evidence and testimony, mostly regarding car thefts and bogus registrations, could be entered as part of the record of the case without witnesses testifying. It was an effort to move the massive case along.

Even with the move, the trial entered its second month with an endless parade of witnesses discussing car thefts. Legendary moonshine buster and U.S. Marshall W.B. "Big Six" Henderson even made an appearance, telling the court that if one of the missing witnesses didn't show up soon, marshals would be dispatched to find him.

One of the last prosecution witnesses was a Louisville man, Fontis Emberton, who was slated to testify about a stolen car he had purchased. Instead, Emberton testified about finding a bomb made of four sticks of dynamite in his car in the weeks leading to trial.

Another witness, Max Bayer, said he had been hired by defendants Shirley Basham and Willie Hudson to "eliminate" Emberton for $5,000. He said the bomb was actually placed in Emberton's car by Melvin Eugene Moore, the man who had been indicted of placing a bomb at the Moody house and who had been killed in a police shootout the previous year.

Finally, after six weeks, the prosecution ended its case. A flurry of motions were then filed by defense attorneys asking that charges against their clients be dismissed, arguing that prosecutors had failed to make a case, with most testimony coming from admitted criminals and liars. Only one defendant succeeded as Judge Swinford ruled that charges should be dropped against Charlotte Mayes, wife of alleged ringleader Billy Mayes. The only testimony relating to her had been someone saying they had seen her riding in a stolen car.

During the lengthy prosecution case, two defendants had changed their pleas to guilty, meaning there were 22 defendants left when the defense case began.

Defense attorneys focused on the credibility, or lack thereof, of prosecution witnesses. They called character witnesses and some of the defendants to the stand to deny the charges in what became a massive game of conflicting statements.

Defendants repeatedly claimed that they did not know the cars they were dealing with were stolen.

News coverage of the case shared space with dispatches from Washington, D.C., about another probe — who was behind a break-in at the Watergate Hotel in that city. While that (soon to be historic) investigation continued, the car theft ring case was — finally — approaching a conclusion.

After eight weeks of testimony, closing statements started on May 22, 1973.

One of the defense attorneys said prosecutors were attacking the very foundations of democracy. He said the symbolic lady of justice "has been bound, gagged, and bludgeoned by the prosecution."

Another said the prosecution's witnesses were "the dregs of humanity."

Finally, the case went to the jury. Despite the massive amount of evidence presented, the jury only took nine hours to deliver verdicts: 19 guilty, three not guilty.

The next day, with a courtroom full of defendant family members, Judge Swinford handed down sentences, with 10 men receiving the maximum sentence of five years in prison and $5,000 fines. The low-end sentences were one year in prison and $1,000 fines.

Some of the family members in the courtroom began crying and one woman even fainted.

Later that week, Darrell Moody's Christmas tree finally came down.

Chapter 15

THE TROOPER

William Barrett, a Tennessee native, was an Air Force veteran when he joined the Tennessee Highway Patrol in the 1960s. After eight years with the THP, with his wife and two young sons in tow, he moved north and joined the Kentucky State Police. He became a road trooper based at Bowling Green's KSP Post 3.

Gary Raymer was a Bowling Green police officer at the time. He recalled that Barrett had an imposing presence that belied a gentle nature.

"He was a great big guy, but a nice fellow," Raymer later said.

He was the kind of cop you wanted on your side in those rough and tumble days when physical attacks on police were not uncommon, Raymer said.

While working in Bowling Green, Barrett befriended a young man named Joe Denning, who in 1969 became Bowling Green's first African-American police officer.

A year later, Denning joined Barrett as a trooper with the KSP.

On Saturday, December 18, 1971, a routine night for Barrett patrolling Warren County included a dinner break about 7 p.m. at Jerry's Diner. There, he met with Denning and both men had a hamburger steak and mashed potatoes before parting ways for the night.

A few hours later, when his 4 p.m.-to-midnight shift ended, Barrett headed home down Russellville Road to the Morehead Trailer Park in Rockfield, where he lived with his wife, Thelma, and two young sons, Mike and Mark. The small trailer park was largely isolated, surrounded mostly by farms, a church and a few scattered houses. With just a sliver of moon in the sky, it was an especially dark night as Barrett made the short trip from Bowling Green.

It was about 15 minutes past midnight when he backed onto a concrete pad that served as a parking spot next to his trailer. As he got out of the cruiser, someone called his name from out of the darkness. The voice came from near a small shed at the back of the property along a fenced tree line. As Barrett spun around toward where his name was called, a double-barreled shotgun blast shattered the still darkness.

Barrett pulled out his revolver and got a shot off at his attacker.

Before he could fire again, the trooper was hit with another shotgun blast. Barrett slumped next to his cruiser, seeping blood. It was there that he died moments later at the age of 35.

His killer, glimpsed by a witness as nothing more than an ominous shape deep in the darkness, made his escape through the trees.

❖❖❖❖❖

Mark Barrett was just 9 at the time. Years later, he told the author he remembers the loud blasts that woke him up that night.

"Why was his mother shooting off fireworks in the middle of the night," he thought. His mother had been shooting off cherry bombs earlier on that December night in 1971, but it was now after midnight. He remembers being puzzled by the sound.

The boy walked into the home's kitchen, where he found his mother sitting in the middle of the floor.

He asked her what was wrong.

"Your dad has been shot," she said.

Denning was at home when the phone rang just past midnight on the morning of December 19, telling him to get back in service because an unnamed law enforcement officer had been fatally shot.

Denning soon learned that the officer who had been killed was his friend, Trooper William Barrett, who he had seen just hours earlier for dinner.

Despite the grief, Denning had a job to do. He joined law enforcement officers from various jurisdictions who spread out across the region for patrols and roadblocks, "looking for any suspicious individuals," Denning said.

Raymer was on duty when the call came in that a trooper had been shot. He raced to the scene at the Morehead Trailer Park and helped keep residents away from the crime scene until more state police arrived.

Meanwhile at the scene, Warren County Coroner J.C. Kirby arrived and took Barrett's body for examination. He said both wounds from the shooting could have been fatal, but it was the chest and shoulder wound from the second shot that apparently caused his death.

Warren County Sheriff Hubert Phelps said at the time that the news of Barrett's killing hit him "like a thunderbolt," and police from his and other agencies quickly volunteered to help the round-the-clock investigation.

Though the roadblocks and patrols failed to yield leads, police quickly zeroed in on a potential suspect. Police learned of a man who purchased a rifle shortly before Barrett's killing and knew Barrett's wife. He was interviewed at length, but police never directly linked him to the crime.

Investigators also looked into arrests Barrett had made, "not only in Kentucky but in Tennessee," Denning recalled.

The day after his death, 170 law enforcement officers from across the region and Lt. Gov. Julian Carroll attended Barrett's funeral service at the J.C. Kirby Funeral Chapel in Bowling Green.

Meanwhile, at Rockfield School — where Barrett's two sons attended — an assembly was held the next week to raise a reward fund for information leading to an arrest in the case.

More than $2,000 was raised, and Commonwealth's Attorney Lowe said the crime was an attack on law enforcement as a whole. Barrett's killer "shot the badge, shot the uniform and shot the symbol of criminal justice and law enforcement," Lowe said.

At the same assembly, the Warren County Automobile Wrecker Drivers group presented small memorial plaques to Barrett's sons.

The ever-growing reward would go unclaimed.

❖❖❖❖❖

Years later, William Barrett's sons discussed the case publicly for the first time with the author.

Mark Barrett remembered that his 6-foot-2, crew-cut father "was always thought of as a big man" and could be "intimidating, but he could be gentle when he wanted to be."

William Barrett was gone a lot for work but made sure he found time to take his boys to their Little League games.

"We were normal kids with a normal childhood," Mark Barrett said.

Mark Barrett remembers that after his mother told him his father had been shot, the night's silence was again pierced by the sound of sirens.

"The next thing I remember, police were everywhere," Mark Barrett said.

Mike Barrett had also been awakened by the gunshots. When he looked out his bedroom window, he saw his father on the ground next to his KSP cruiser. He tried to make sense of the scene.

"I thought he was working on his car," Mike Barrett said.

A neighbor soon came to take the boys away from the house. As they left, the boys "passed our dad's body covered in a sheet," Mark Barrett said.

A few months after the murder, Thelma took her boys back home to family in Tennessee and eventually remarried.

"We went on living our lives as best we could," Mark Barrett said.

The decades passed.

While Mike and Mark knew the case was active and were regularly invited back to Kentucky for memorial events for fallen troopers, the case was more of a memory than a mission.

That changed in 2019.

William Barrett's murder, and that of a man named Larry Key (see next chapter), was detailed in a four-part series, "The Ambush Killings," in the *Daily News* that year.

Mike Barrett was on vacation in Grand Cayman when his brother sent him a link to the articles.

"It brought back some crazy memories," Mike Barrett said. "You don't get over it, you get through it."

It also shed, for the brothers, new light on the murder of their father.

"My head was spinning" with new details about their father's case, Mike Barrett said.

It also brought a new desire to see justice.

Chapter 16

THE WITNESS

Larry Stinson Key grew up in Edmonson County, the youngest of nine children. At Sunfish High School, he excelled at sports and was offered a chance to head to California and try out to join the Los Angeles Dodgers system, but chose instead to stay home.

He married his high school sweetheart, Renetta, in 1960. Two sons soon followed — Todd was born in 1961 and Brad in 1966.

Decades later, Todd Key remembers his father as a charismatic man.

"People gravitated toward him," he said.

"He was a great father," Brad Key said. "He was very kind and very generous with his friends and family."

He also passed on his passion for baseball to his oldest son.

"He taught me how to throw a curveball," Todd Key said.

"We were poor, but we were happy," Renetta recalled.

In 1971, Larry Key started working at Cave City Truck Stop on U.S. 31-W just outside Bowling Green. Soon, he was bringing home more money than would be expected from someone pumping gas and filling tires with air.

"He wouldn't say where it was coming from," said Renetta, who felt it wasn't her place to press him on it and instead focused on raising her sons in a simple but fulfilling life.

"With two young boys, I took care of my children, my home and my husband," she said.

Then, on November 13, 1971, the family returned from church to their Glendale home to find a yard full of police officers.

"It came crashing down very, very hard," Renetta recalled of her previously quiet life.

Larry Key was arrested, taken to jail in Louisville and charged in federal court along with two other men with the possession and sale of drugs – activities that allegedly were taking place at the truck stop.

Suddenly, the source of the extra income became clear.

"It was a very difficult, emotional time because our life changed forever," Renetta said.

Even after Larry Key was freed on bail to await his trial, "there was a lot of tension, a lot of stress," Renetta said, but the family was "hoping for the best."

Those hopes were brutally eliminated on July 28, 1972.

Renetta recalled it was an especially hot and muggy day when Larry Key left for work. As the time for him to come home approached, Renetta sent Todd and Brad, then 11 and 5, respectively, to pick up some bread at a nearby store and wait for their father passing by to catch a ride home.

They came back alone.

"They had just walked through the door when I got a phone call from a friend in Sonora who had a police scanner and she had heard that there had been a shooting," Renetta said.

She took the boys to a bedroom and started praying that their father and husband were safe.

"Then the police started coming, and it was chaos," she said.

Decades later, she learned from police many of the details of her husband's death.

As he was turning off Interstate 65 at the Glendale exit to come home, Larry Key pulled over to the side of the exit ramp. Two men in a two-tone green car who were following Key pulled up behind him. They exited the vehicle and approached Key's car.

Shouting was heard.

As the men got to the car, one on each side, the man on the driver's side of Key's car pulled out a .38-caliber handgun and shot Key in the face. Despite being shot, Larry Key pushed past the shooter and started running toward I-65. Before he could make it, another shot hit him in the back and pierced his heart. He died in the grass alongside the exit ramp.

It was the day after Larry Key's 31st birthday.

Four witnesses saw his killing just off the Interstate 65 exit ramp in Glendale. Two Indiana couples, returning north from a Florida vacation, were nearby dealing with car troubles. They gave general descriptions of the two men involved and their vehicle.

Upon hearing the description of the vehicle, Key's wife Renetta recalled seeing a car matching that description near her house an hour before the shooting, and a neighbor reported seeing one of the men in the car looking into the Key garage.

In hindsight, Renetta said she believes the men were planning to kill Larry Key at his home, but perhaps arrived an hour early after a mix-up involving different time zones.

But despite the eyewitnesses, the Key case also went unsolved.

Through *Daily News* articles, the Barretts made contact with Renetta.

Renetta and her sons offered a substantial reward for information, paid for a billboard spotlighting the cases, established a Facebook page dedicated to the murders and have been investigating the case on their own.

"Her resilience to not let this die down caused us to reevaluate our position," Mike Barrett said.

The brothers became more active in lobbying law enforcement to pursue the case.

They also believe that their father's murder may be linked to the Key murder and possible law enforcement corruption at the time.

It was only when they read the *Daily News* articles that they discovered that their father had been working undercover for law enforcement.

In hindsight, "it seemed like he was gone a lot," Mark Barrett said, but their father never discussed his activities at home.

"It was almost like a double life," Mike Barrett said.

Over the years, evidence from the cases has gone missing, according to Wilson, and corruption among some in law enforcement at the time has come to light.

"It leads you to believe there was a cover-up at the time," Mike Barrett said.

Chapter 17

A LINK?

Officials at the time did not publicly link the cases of the killings of Trooper Barrett and Larry Key, although there was a common denominator in that both Barrett and Key were privy to drug activity at the area's truck stops.

Barrett was also looking into wrongdoing by others in law enforcement at the time he was killed.

Law enforcement sources don't discount the theory that the cases are linked.

Confirmation that Barrett was in the thick of investigating criminal activity at truck stops, such as the one Key worked at and was reportedly providing information about, comes in the form of court records that show, for example, that in 1970 he went undercover and purchased amphetamines at a truck stop in Barren County.

The truck stop operator was subsequently charged and convicted of possessing with the intent to sell 43,100 amphetamine pills and was sentenced to five years in prison.

Key, after his arrest, offered what is known as a proffer. Presumably in exchange for some leniency in his prosecution, Key was offering to testify as to what he knew about the area drug trade.

"I believe in my father's proffer that he was going to … identify a Kentucky state trooper who he knew, and we now know for a fact, was dealing narcotics himself," Todd Key said. The family believes this former state trooper was working for Larry Key's family members involved in illegal activity. Barrett was alleged to also have knowledge of the former state trooper's criminal activity.

Drug dealing was the latest crime to thrive in southcentral Kentucky in the Little Chicago era, one that was especially hard on those in law enforcement.

Former Bowling Green Police Department officer and chief Gary Raymer said some of the rougher men in town viewed attacking a police officer as "a sport."

Much of the criminal activity at the time was based at truck stops. Many truckers were "using speed and amphetamines to keep them awake," said Tommie Smith, who worked at the time with the Kentucky State Police and Warren County Sheriff's Office.

Truck stops were also convenient places to arrange transportation of drugs and stolen items and provided a steady customer base for the prostitutes who also worked there.

Those involved in criminal activity had no qualms about killing witnesses, bombing rivals and even targeting those in law enforcement.

Some believe that corruption in state law enforcement may have prevented a quick solution to the Barrett and Key killings.

As evidence to that allegation, Renetta later pointed to a reporter the involvement of a man named Harold Brown with the investigation into her husband's death.

Brown worked in the state office of the federal Drug Enforcement Agency. He was found dead in his Louisville home in 1984 from an apparent suicide, but some officials at the time questioned that determination.

"There are people around who wouldn't have minded shooting him," then-Jefferson County Coroner Richard Greathouse told United Press International in 1984.

Brown was under investigation and surveillance at the time of his death by the Jefferson and Meade County sheriff's offices and the KSP for suspected activities in narcotics and his involvement in a company selling poisons, according to the UPI story. The *Chicago Tribune* also reported at the time that Brown was being investigated for his alleged involvement in international drug smuggling.

Renetta said she believes in hindsight that Brown, allegedly working with drug dealers, was part of the effort to thwart the investigation into her husband's death.

As for the belief that the Larry Key and William Barrett killings are linked, a strange event at a local resort a few months before her husband was shot cemented Renetta's belief that those responsible for her husband's death also killed Barrett.

Her husband was working the 3-to-11 p.m. shift January 24, 1972, at the Cave City truck stop. He was free on a bond after his arrest on drug charges two months earlier.

"He was very punctual about getting home," Renetta said. "But by midnight, he was still not there."

"This was totally out of character," she said. She began making calls, including to police, but nobody seemed to know where Larry Key was.

He finally stumbled home about 5:30 a.m.

"He was very emaciated looking, pale, totally out of character," Renetta said. Larry Key told his wife he had gone out drinking with a friend. Later, he approached her "and got down on his knees, which was totally out of character, and said, 'If you'll forgive me, I'll spend the rest of my life making it up to you and the boys.'"

But Renetta said she learned only years later from police sources that Larry Key's account of the night "was not the truth," she said.

Renetta said police sources told her Larry Key had been drugged that night by people he had been having drinks with. In his incapacitated state, he was taken to a room at the Park Mammoth Resort in Park City. Video and photos were taken of him with a female in compromising positions and then they "tried to get him to say that he had murdered trooper William H. Barrett out of Post 3 in Bowling Green ... and not testify in court" regarding his drug case.

Renetta said police showed her a photo from that night of her husband and the woman.

Larry Key never discussed the events of that night with Renetta before he was killed that July. A relative, however, told her that before his death, Larry Key had told him that if Renetta ever found out what had happened that night, that he should let Renetta know that he was not there by choice.

Renetta said the only reason someone would have to get her husband to "confess" to killing Barrett was if they were involved in the trooper's murder — "I think we can assume that for sure," she said.

Renetta and her sons believed those involved in the drug trade, from Larry Key's family members to corrupt members of law enforcement, were looking to take care of two problems with Larry Key's death: They would not have to worry about his potential testimony against them, and they could pin the death of Barrett on Larry Key.

After the blackmail attempt failed, Renetta and her sons believe the killing of their husband and father included a plan to plant a shotgun in Larry Key's car.

"They were going to link him to the Barrett murder by planting that shotgun," Todd Key said, but the plan was foiled by the presence of the four witnesses who were dealing with a broken-down vehicle on the Interstate 65 Glendale exit ramp where Larry Key was shot and killed.

Even decades later, the two killings remain on the minds of many in southcentral Kentucky.

Smith had started working for the Kentucky State Police in 1989. He was on administrative duty at Post 3 in 1990 when the Barrett report first came across his desk.

"I read it cover to cover," Smith said.

He believes the crime was clearly a planned execution.

"Whoever did it had some idea of his schedule ... they also called him by his name when they shot him," Smith said.

Smith went to Texas, Florida, and Minnesota to talk to people who might have information regarding the case. But no break came, and time is the enemy of justice.

As for the theory that the killings of Key and Barrett are linked: "From the outside looking in, it could be possible ... a lot of it makes sense," Smith said.

Raymer was on patrol the night Barrett was shot. He also believes it was a well-orchestrated murder.

"From my perspective, whoever did it was a professional," Raymer said. "It was an intentional hit."

"A shotgun is not only a deadly weapon, it is largely untraceable," said Raymer, who also believes at least two people were involved: the shooter and the driver of a getaway car.

They knew the area well enough to drive away without arousing suspicion, he said.

In both the Key and Barrett cases, there are no publicly named suspects or persons of interest. One person, however, has been identified by several sources as possibly being involved in their deaths. The person is a former member of law enforcement who still lives in southcentral Kentucky. The individual has links to both Barrett and Key and was allegedly working with the drug dealers who may be responsible for their deaths.

As of 2025, the person has not been charged or publicly named by law enforcement as a suspect or person of interest in either case.

EPILOGUE

Eventually, crime rates in Bowling Green and across Kentucky began to diminish.

Concerted efforts to root out corruption, prosecute criminal syndicates and improved law enforcement made a difference — although new challenges would continue to surface.

Today, Bowling Green is known as one of the fastest-growing and economically successful cities in the state, while Newport draws countless families to area tourist attractions such as the Newport Aquarium.

Remnants of the darker era, however, can still be spotted, as in a few surviving bars in downtown Newport that once were "Sin City" hot spots, and a sliver of cracked blacktop in Bowling Green that was once the infamous Burke's Alley.

But the era primarily lives on in memories, black and white photos, and faded newspaper articles. Most of the murders chronicled on these pages remain unsolved and will likely remain so. That doesn't, of course, stop speculation, and for families who lost a loved one, a hope for long-sought resolution to the crimes that marked a dark chapter of Kentucky history, when the Bluegrass ran red.

ACKNOWLEDGEMENTS

While there have been countless individuals who have helped with this project in one way or another, special thanks go to the helpful staffs at the Logan and Warren County libraries and Western Kentucky University Special Collections, the many individuals who graciously agreed to be interviewed, the *Russellville News Democrat & Leader* and *Cincinnati Enquirer* for use of their photos, and the many readers and supporters of my first book, *The Cemetery Road Murders*, who encouraged this project.

The wonderful staff at Acclaim Press, the *Bowling Green Daily News* and myriad unnamed folks who helped with this project also deserve a sincere thank you.

And, of course, sincere thanks go to my family for pardoning the many occasions when writing and research interfered with time with them.

BIBLIOGRAPHY

Periodicals

Associated Press
Bowling Green Daily News
Bowling Green Democrat
Chicago Tribune
Cincinnati Enquirer
Cincinnati Magazine
Inside Detective Magazine
Kentucky Post
Lexington Herald
Lexington Leader
Life Magazine
Look Magazine
Louisville Courier Journal
Nashville Banner
Nashville Tennessean
New York Times
Northern Kentucky Tribune
Owensboro Messenger
Russellville News Democrat
Saga Magazine
The Kentucky Post
The Logan Leader
The Northerner
The Rambler
Time Magazine
True Detective Magazine
United Press International

Books

A New History of Kentucky. The University Press of Kentucky, 1997.

Album of Early Bowling Green Kentucky Landmarks. NP, 1978.

Asher, Brad. *Kentucky*. Interlink Books, 2007.

Baird, Nancy, Crowe-Carraco, Carroll, and Morse, Michael. *Bowling Green A Pictorial History*. The Donning Company, 1983.

Barker, Thomas; Potter, Gary; Meglen, Jenna. *Wicked Newport*. The History Press, 2008.

Dickey, Robert. *Greyhound to Vegas*. St. Margaret Publishers, ND.

Futrell, Roger H. *Peach Orchard Road*. Bookworld Communications Corp., 1975.

Higdon III, James. *The Cornbread Mafia*. Lyons Press. 2012.

Lawson, Robert G. *Who Killed Betty Gail Brown*. University Press of Kentucky, 2017.

Swietek, Wes. T*he Cemetery Road Murders*. Acclaim Press, 2020.

ABOUT THE AUTHOR

Wes Swietek is an award-winning journalist who has served as editor of newspapers in Illinois, Georgia, Tennessee, and Kentucky. A Chicago native, he is currently the managing editor of the *Daily News* in Bowling Green, Kentucky, where he lives with his wife and two children.

This is his second book. His first book was *The Cemetery Road Murders* about an infamous murder case in Bowling Green.

INDEX